KABLUK OF THE ESKIMO

by
LOWELL THOMAS

WITH 17 ILLUSTRATIONS

KABLUK OF
THE ESKIMO

KABLUK OF THE ESKIMO

Frontispiece

CONTENTS

CHAPTER		PAGE
I.	IN EVERY LATITUDE THERE IS A STORY-TELLER	9
II.	A PARISIAN MEETS A PATRIARCH OF THE NORTH	16
III.	DRIFTING TOWARD THE AURORA BOREALIS	21
IV.	RIDING THE TEMPEST WITH UTIK AND THE "WHITE MAN"	26
V.	I WAS A FRENCHMAN. I BECOME AN ESKIMO	35
VI.	THEY OFFER ME NORRAK, THE BLONDE GIRL OF THE TRIBE	45
VII.	A YEAR ALONE ON LOON ISLAND	58
VIII.	AI'VUK THE WALRUS	74
IX.	THE ATTACK OF THE KAYAKS	88
X.	KUBLO GOES TO AURORA BOREALIS	101
XI.	"THE SILLY FRIVOLITIES THAT MAKE YOU LONG FOR THE GAIETY OF PARIS"	113
XII.	THE HUNT FOR NANUK, THE GREAT WHITE BEAR	127
XIII.	THIS WOMAN HAS KILLED NANUK	138
XIV.	FAR SOUTH ON HUDSON BAY MY WOMAN WAITS	148
XV.	ANGEKOK AND THE CARIBOU	163
XVI.	ANOTINOAK, THE TUSKED ONE, AND HIS BATTLE WITH THE WOLVES	181

CONTENTS

CHAPTER		PAGE
XVII.	A MESSENGER FROM THE LAND OF THE MUSK OX	196
XVIII.	THE WORLD HAS GONE CRAZY	208
XIX.	FROM ICE TO FIRE	227
XX.	MY FATHER, I HAVE CHANGED	242
XXI.	AKPEK, THE CHIEF, DEPARTS FOR AURORA BOREALIS	249
XXII.	SO THE STORY ENDS	254

ILLUSTRATIONS

Kabluk of the Eskimo - - - FRONTISPIECE	
	PAGE
He led me over the snow to a newly made igloo	12
"When do you leave for the hunt?" - - -	40
Busiest of all were the women - - - -	48
The woman is really dealing with her father's soul —so whatever the boy wants to do his mother must permit - - - - - -	56
Bride and bridegroom in the happy village beneath the Northern Lights - - - - -	80
Stepping into their kayaks the walrus hunters glided swiftly away - - - - - -	88
After the battle with Ai'vuk the walrus, the Children of the North array themselves for the triumphal dance - - - - -	96
The women were quiet and fearful - - -	104
While Akpek hunts Nanuk, the great white bear, Nayume, his wife, goes fishing - - -	128
Eskimo archers aiming their arrows at Nanuk, the great white bear - - - - -	136
What the well-dressed woman wears at the blubber banquet - - - - - - -	144
The machine age in Eskimo land - - -	168
Off for a summer resort - - - - -	192
Finally the blizzard passed - - - - -	200
When the War was over I returned to Akpek's village on the fringe of the frozen sea - -	248

Kabluk of the Eskimo

CHAPTER I

IN EVERY LATITUDE THERE IS A STORY-TELLER

THE friendship of Kabluk, the white man, and Akpek, the Eskimo chief, constitutes a singular story of a profound human relation. It's the Damon and Pythias theme transferred to the dim hyperboreal North, a David and Jonathan tale set in a distant world of ice, igloos, and giant hunts.

To say that the North is a place of great stories is trite, banal, but also perfectly true. In my callow days I visited Alaska and filled myself with a juvenile enthusiasm for rugged Arctic lands, racy, granitic characters, and life in the raw. It was all as described in the books, and I formed an ideal of the men of the North lands quite in accordance with the customary tradition of Northern stories.

I recall Humpbacked Jake and Whiskey Nels, two characters as rough and individual as their names. They were fishermen who followed the salmon runs up and down the Alaskan coast. When I knew them, they were operating a ship out of Cordova, and I spent a week or so with them while they caught millions of salmon, the "humpies" that happened to be running.

Great story-tellers were Humpbacked Jake and Whiskey Nels. At night in the cabin of the fishing schooner they told me tales of their adventures in Alaska. They had followed nearly every gold-rush and, never striking pay dirt, they had always returned to their old profession of fishing. They were tall-story-tellers too, but you could never tell just where the real left off and the tall part of it began. Take this one which Whiskey Nels related with an immense gusto:

"Late one afternoon, in the days when I was prospecting along the Kuskokwim, I was returning to my cabin. I had been panning all day and for once had forgotten to take along my rifle. I noticed a bear following me. When I hurried, he hurried. I ran as hard as I could and just got to my cabin in the nick of time. I jumped inside, bolted the door, and seized my rifle from the peg. Presently, when I looked out of the window, I saw the bear with his head sticking up above a log.

"In those days I had the reputation of being a dead shot. I fired and down went the bear's head. But a moment later up it came again. I was madder than hell that I had missed. I fired again and down it went. But a moment later up it came again. In fact, that bear stuck his head up nine times and I shot nine

STORY-TELLER

times before he would keep it down. I was disgusted with my shooting.

"The next morning I went out and looked. There erew nine bears lying dead behind that log."

As Whiskey Nels finished his story, Humpbacked Jake stroked his whiskers and roared with laughter. Then he said he had had a somewhat similar experience. And Jake told this one:

"I was out on the creek one day and I too had forgotten my rifle. That night on my way back to camp I saw a bear following me, and I ran as hard as I could. But that bear was catching up with me. There were no trees anywhere that I could climb. Just as I was about to drop from exhaustion I saw a lone tree up ahead.

"When I got under it I found that the lowest limb was twenty feet off the ground. Well, I made a great jump——"

At this point I excitedly broke in and asked:

"Did you make it?"

To which Jake replied:

"Well, I didn't catch it going up, but I caught it coming down."

Humpbacked Jake and Whiskey Nels were known to all the fishermen from Ketchikan to Dutch Harbour. But I recall two far more widely known characters in the North. Every white man and every Indian knew them—in fact, had known them over a period of some twenty-five years. One was Bishop Rowe, famous for his piety. The other was Malamute Bill, famous for his profanity. In fact, Bill's flow of sulphurous language was the admiration of the Yukon.

Although each knew of the other by reputation, and their trails had crossed a hundred times, yet in all those twenty-five years they had never met.

Bishop Rowe told me the story of the time when the meeting finally did take place. It was a memorable occasion when the two men, so opposite in fame, finally found themselves face to face. The Bishop is one of the great yarn-spinners of the North and I can only give a faint impression of the unction with which he related the anecdote.

One day the Bishop was on his way to the "outside" from the Yukon Valley. It was in midwinter and a blizzard was raging. After crossing the great tundra plain of interior Alaska, the Bishop entered the first mountain-pass. It had been snowing for days. The churchman saw a man and dog-team coming from the opposite direction. The Bishop didn't recognize the dog-team driver, and the dog-team driver didn't recognize the Bishop. Both were muffled in furs, and under the circumstances a man might not recognize his own brother. When the newcomer's sled drew up alongside they stopped and the Bishop innocently asked:

"Well, pard, how's the trail down your way?"

And then the church dignitary knew that he had

HE LED ME OVER THE SNOW TO A NEWLY MADE IGLOO

Courtesy National Museum of Canada

STORY-TELLER

finally met Malamute Bill. For days that master of blazing prose had been waiting for a chance to express himself on the subject of the trail. The Bishop told me that in all his life he had never heard such a stream of purple language. Bill cursed every mile of the trail, every dog in his team, every hair on every dog's back, and the ancestors of all his dogs.

Finally, completely exhausted, he sat down on his sledge and asked:

"And how's the trail up your way?"

To which the Bishop gave his classic reply:

"You've expressed my sentiments exactly!"

These were story-tellers of the North to whose talented yarn-spinning I listened during those early Alaskan travels of mine, when I saw the frozen lands with the sort of vision you find in a current juvenile.

Years later, I was in the town of Edmonton, in Canada. There was none of the customary circumstance, no sitting around the campfire or passing long hours in an Arctic shack, or watching the huskies feed at a stop along the trail. It was at a luncheon of business men, ordinary, commonplace. Nor did the speaker have the seeming of a droll, hard-bitten character of the North. He was rugged enough, a powerfully built, middle-aged man, ruddy of face, dark hair, greyeyed. He looked the part of a Frenchman, like one of those sturdy and often stolid men you see in the country districts of France. And he spoke with a rich

KABLUK OF THE ESKIMO

French accent, a kind of English that was filled with the idioms of the North but at the same time bookish. He was a man of education, you could see, cultured in an Old World sense.

He made a speech at that Board of Trade meeting, and the way he began caught my quick attention. He pointed to a chart on the wall.

"Your map of Canada here," he said, "will not help me. Because the part I want to tell you about is off the map, above it, farther north."

And then, with his curious French accent and with a constant seeking for the right word, he told of the northern shore of the Labrador Peninsula, of the fur trade there, and of the Eskimos.

The Eskimos called him Kabluk. Among the white men he was Louis Romanet.

Beside this Frenchman of the Arctics, those other story-tellers of the North seemed just a trifle stagy. Their stories, their personalities, were built according to the pattern of the books. In Louis Romanet there is the novelty of a simplicity and a fervour. He is a sensitive Frenchman with an æsthetic cast of mind, who sees the North with an amount of delicate perception of which our standard pioneer type of Anglo-Saxon adventurer could not be capable. You might say that this man Romanet looks at things in a way that is not in accordance with the books; or, rather, you may say that he sees them with a perception schooled, not in

STORY-TELLER

Bret Harte or Jack London, but in the classic French tradition of Voltaire and Renan. He had written many notes of lovely Old World flavour. It seemed to me that here was a man of great adventures who had seen the North with a vision that was different.

I got his story from him and found that it was no mere string of Northern experiences, no mere rambling tale of adventures in the Arctic. It was a dramatic story of a friendship, a deeply emotional tale of a brotherly tie between two men, between Kabluk, the white man, and Akpek, the Eskimo chief. And Romanet told the tale with an amount of brimming emotion, open and ingenuous, such as is possible to a man of Gaelic race and tradition.

CHAPTER II

A PARISIAN MEETS A PATRIARCH OF THE NORTH

THERE were big storms in September, and then the spell of the Arctic night and ice settled down upon the North. Winter came early that year. There were three of us in the post on the Koksoak River, trading in furs for Revillon Frères of Paris. Ours was a new post. We had come up from Quebec in July, and had spent the remainder of the short summer in putting up a couple of frame shacks, one for our living quarters and the other for storage and trade. Our post, which we called "The Fort", was near the northern tip of the Labrador Peninsula. We were twenty-five miles up river from Ungava Bay, on Hudson Strait.

A few Eskimos came drifting along our way soon after we had arrived. They came just as debris floats and gathers in an eddy of a stream. They were loafers, worthless fellows, such as are always attracted to a fur-trading post. The other Eskimos despised them and called them "White Men" because of their worthlessness. These "White Men" of the North helped us build our houses and then they hung around as permanent parasites, doing odd jobs—getting wood, running errands, carrying burdens—the coolie jobs. They were our only companions during the winter months, as the real Eskimos and Indians did not begin to come in until the next trading season. Winter closed down and we were alone with our hangers-on, the worthless "White Men".

In the post we kept our standards of living as best we could. We had plenty of provisions. We ate well and slept well, played cards and sang songs, drank good Canadian whisky, talked about our home towns in Europe, and wished we were there.

My two companions were old hands at fur trading in the North. Yvon Drollet was the boss; next in command was Raoul Thevenet; and I, as the greenhorn of the outfit, came third. It was my first experience in the North. I had never been among the Eskimos before, and I was eager to learn their ways. I made friends with those loafers, the "White Men" around the post.

When they were sick, I went out of my way to do what I could for them. We had some medicine; and I knew as much about sickness as common sense taught me. It was sufficient. I helped them a little and they began to regard me respectfully as a doctor—a medicine man, a miracle-working shaman. I learned what I could from them regarding the ways of their people, but it was not much. They had been among aliens so much that they had forgotten their tribal lore and they no longer cared for anything but the passing moment.

There was one amongst them who was not so bad. He was not a real loafer, not really a "White Man". Utik was an orphan, a waif. He didn't go with the tribe, because he had no tribe. He had no partners for the hunt; yet he was bright and brave and with half a chance he would have made a good Eskimo. He attached himself to me and from him I learned my first few words of the Eskimo language.

I look back upon that winter of long ago now, and I can see that it was only a time of waiting for me. It was an interval of nothingness. I had not begun to live as yet. I did not know the North; I knew nothing, understood nothing. I was like a man in a drowsy daze just before he is fully awake.

One night, Utik came to my bed and shook me awake. From the few words he spoke I gathered that there was somebody sick, someone who was in need of immediate attention. I got up and followed him outside. The night was cold and clear, with a silver crescent moon on the northern horizon, and I shivered as he led me over the snow to a newly made igloo a short distance away. We crawled through the narrow tunnel-like opening on our hands and knees, and shoving aside the hide that hid the inner chamber from view, I stood up. I glanced around the chamber. Half of it was occupied by a semicircular shelf of ice, and upon it was a pallet of caribou hides, and soft mats of the same kind were scattered about. It was occupied by a couple and their little girl. The people within it were newcomers, a family travelling from one place to another. They were not loafers, they were not the despised Eskimo "White Men".

An old man greeted me with a single word; "*Chimo,*" he said. In the Arctic it is a word of many meanings. It means welcome. It means a handshake. It means all the polite things that go with a courteous, civilized greeting. There was something stately and dignified about the Eskimo patriarch, something indicating that he was a great man among his people.

The Eskimo was about sixty years old; tall and alert, with an energetic face that bore a tinge of sadness. He was of medium height and powerfully built, with a stocky torso set on slightly undersized legs, and long arms. The hood of his caribou parka was thrown back, revealing a mat of thick, coarse, black hair heavily shot with grey; and it hung down to the bottom of his ears, where it was cut in a straight line. His eyes were small and slightly slanting; under a flat nose his open mouth displayed a set of uneven teeth; and through the deep bronze of his skin the tattoo marks of his youth still showed faintly. He wore a clipped, pointed beard that accentuated the nobility of his bearing. His name was Akpek, I learned, and he was the chief of his tribe.

He pointed to a child who lay moaning on the

KABLUK OF THE ESKIMO

pallet of caribou skins. With Utik acting as interpreter, I learned that old Akpek had heard about the white medicine man and his magic; he had turned from his path so that I could relieve the child. I looked at the girl and from the talk and the gestures I gathered that she was suffering from some kind of indigestion. Cramps, I thought.

I gave her a strong purgative and told them perhaps she would be better when morning came. As I left, the patriarchal Eskimo again spoke only one word, "*Chimo.*" It is a word that also means gratitude and farewell. The Eskimo have few words in their language, but each word means many things—when used with a different intonation.

Luckily my prophecy was correct and next day the little girl was sliding around on the ice and laughing as Eskimo children usually do, while the elders prepared for their departure. Before leaving, Chief Akpek came to see me. He told me that his tribe lived far away—across the ice to the north of the island of Akpatok—and he asked me to visit him some time in his village. Then once more he spoke that expressive word, "*Chimo.*"

The sun was nearing its highest point when Chief Akpek and his little band of Eskimos started across the ice; they turned downstream, following the course of the Koksoak River; and I watched them until they disappeared over the white horizon.

CHAPTER III

DRIFTING TOWARD THE AURORA BOREALIS

I AM the seventh son of a carpenter. I was born in the south-east of France, at St. Nazaire-en-Royan, near the boundary of Italy. My birthplace is in a beautiful little valley, sunny, warm, and southern, among high mountains. From the place of my birth, you might think me more likely to become a wanderer of the tropics than of the frigid Northland. In the sunshine-bathed vale, covered with pretty blue flowers, my brothers and sisters and I had gay times together.

My mother died when I was so young that I do not remember her at all. My father was poor and I grew up rather like a little savage. Then my father died and my six brothers and I were left homeless.

As a veteran of the Crimean War, my father was entitled to have two of his children educated at the expense of the Government. And so it was that I was sent with a brother to an orphan school near Paris. There I received a military education and in time advanced from private to corporal, and then to sergeant. I studied hard to qualify as a commissioned officer. In due time I was a sprightly young lieutenant, swaggering around in a new uniform, with a lovely damsel on my arm; and I did my share of devilry, drinking and gambling with my brother officers. The people of my family were good, solid, working folks, and they were proud to have a relative who was an officer. They looked forward to a day when they could be proud in the possession of a colonel, possibly a general, in the family.

But there was something wild in me; something unruly in my make-up. The honest, simple virtue of obedience and the routine of my duties began to irk me. There were rumours about opportunities in Canada for Frenchmen who cared to go into the far North. I listened and investigated. The far North, where opportunity beckoned, was up around the Gulf of St. Lawrence. To this day I don't know just what it was that caused me to break away. Perhaps it was some vague premonition that in the Arctic I would be a bad man no longer; that on the shores of the Arctic Sea I would acquire goodness of heart and peace. Anyway, I went. I resigned from the Army with the rank of Lieutenant of Reserves. My family didn't like it, for now they would have no general, nor even a colonel, in the family. They were mad and they cursed my folly.

On the ship, *La Savoy*, bound for New York, were a number of French priests and nuns. It was during the time that the French Government was abolishing the religious congregations, and these priests and nuns

THE AURORA BOREALIS

were going into exile in the land whither I was bound. But they were happy. They sang all day, because they were going to old Quebec and they knew that they would receive a hearty welcome there. In them there was already a great love for Canada and I got my first real enthusiasm for the land of my adoption from them.

I landed in New York with just five dollars in my pocket, a sum quite insufficient to carry me on to Quebec, as I immediately discovered. So I had to hustle around and find a job in New York. For a while I washed dishes in a restaurant for my board and lodging. Later I polished glasses in a saloon.

In New York I longed for Quebec with a great longing. I talked little English, and I was miserable and depressed while I was saving the pennies that were to carry me on my way. In Quebec, I knew, everybody spoke French and I somehow imagined that would ease my heart; but now I realize that I was discontent and melancholy because there was some devil in me that would not let me rest easy.

Finally, I had enough money for railroad fare to the city of my dreams, and it was not long before I was looking out the window of a railway coach as the train neared the world-famous bluff that is Quebec.

To me, Quebec was like another bit of France, but still I was unable to find happiness. If I hadn't enough goodness in me to be joyful in my own France, how could this alien French city in the New World give me that something which I lacked? I was uneasy with discontent, yet I did not have the least idea what I craved, what I needed.

Happy or not, one must live, and by merest chance I found a job in a storage warehouse belonging to Revillon Frères, the famous fur people. I got five dollars a week for sweeping the floors and I thought it good pay. The raw fur fascinated me. I was always sneaking into the bins to examine the pelts. I would fondle them and study them, wondering what the lives of the animals that had borne them might have been.

That was my sole pleasure. It amused me to study the furs of different kinds. I soon became skilful in picking them out, in learning their markings, and in detecting the various grades. My bosses noticed my interest, and one day my immediate superior asked:

"How would you like to go into the North, *mon ami*? Do you want a job at a fur-trading post?"

I had not thought of that, but there was no peace or contentment in me and I was willing to go anywhere to get away from myself, so I answered briefly: "Yes." I did not guess that I was destined to find up there in the ice and snow, under the eerie glow of the aurora borealis, the goodness of heart that I needed.

One bright July morning in 1903 the steamship *Stord* entered the Gulf of St. Lawrence and stood away to the north, bound for Hudson Strait and Ungava Bay. The vessel rolled on the great swells as we passed along the bleak, rock-ribbed Newfoundland coast. Entering sub-Arctic waters, the *Stord* wallowed on her way cautiously, for we were in uncharted seas. From time to time we encountered icebergs, huge scintillating masses of ice glistening in the sunshine, towering fully two hundred feet into the air. Magnificent sights they presented.

The perpetual daylight of the Arctic had a peculiar effect on our nerves and we became cranky. It was impossible to sleep because of the heat, and our tempers were not improved by snow blindness, resulting from the intense glare of the sun on the sparkling water and ice.

We entered the ice pack, ploughing through a narrow channel that ran north-westward. The opening was filled with small cakes of candled ice which collapsed into thousands of sharp fragments when struck by the prow of the advancing *Stord*. On either hand the ice field extended for untold leagues. Conditions favoured us, and in a few days we were in open water at the entrance to Hudson Strait. The time had come to bear south, into Ungava Bay.

And so it was that I came to "The Fort" on the Koksoak River. With the coming of winter, life at the post settled down. We waited for the trading season which would come with the summer. I had a desire to learn the ways of the men of the North. Utik served as my mentor, and with the coming of the big snows it was from him that I first learned how to handle a team of huskies.

CHAPTER IV

RIDING THE TEMPEST WITH UTIK AND THE "WHITE MAN"

As time went on, the days became long and dreary, and in "The Fort" we had to make every effort to keep from losing our spirits in the long Arctic night. At first I slept away the greater part of the day, because there was no night for sleeping nor day for waking.

When we were not sleeping we talked and talked; we played at cards for days at a time; and we read over our books time and again. The days went ceaselessly by, seemingly without beginning or end. Daily I was out with the dog-team and, under Utik's expert tutelage, I learned to handle a sledge with the best of them.

"*Allons!*" I said to my companions. "I think I will go for a visit to the village of Akpek, the chief."

"It is no trip for a greenhorn," said Thevenet, shaking his head.

"*Oui*," agreed Drollet; "it will be a difficult journey."

"But it is good business," I urged. "Besides, I do not go alone. I go with Utik and another."

"So be it," assented the factor. "When do you leave?"

RIDING THE TEMPEST

"In the morning."

"*Allons!*" cried Thevenet. "To bed, *mon enfant*. You will need your beauty sleep."

I was up early, but Utik and his companion were earlier. The two *komutiks* were ready for the trail when I went outside. Each was drawn by a team of ten dogs. The huskies, wearing their new harness, were a lively sight. They were anxious to be on the go, and they howled joyously in their impatience for the start. Saying adieu to my companions, I took my place in the sledge handled by Utik.

"*Huit*—go!" he shouted.

The sledges jumped forward. The howling ceased and red tongues hung out. The shaggy backs strained at the traces and nervous legs skimmed over the icy ground as the dogs raced along, heads down, their bushy tails stuck out straight behind.

Utik handled the lead team and his companion followed at a short distance to the rear. I sat at ease with my legs stretched out. By my side Utik trotted, steering the sledge with little pushes and jerks in the desired direction. At intervals he seated himself at the front of the *komutik*, with his head and body facing forward and his legs hanging over one side. He held the whip downward so the lash trailed on the snow.

The whip was more than thirty feet long and it was every bit as wicked as it looked. It was very large at the grip, gradually narrowing down to a single line, where it terminated in the lash. Native ability and constant practice had made Utik astonishingly skilful with his whip. It was amazing the way he would flick an ear of his lead dog time after time.

Fixing his eye on the dog's ear, he would bring forward the handle of his whip and then jerk it back, short, with a circular motion of his arm upward; the long line, moving with the motion of the handle, accelerated its speed as it whistled through the air, and the lash invariably clipped the ear, and then followed a shrill yelp of pain.

"*Harra—harra!*" snorted Utik, snapping his whip in emphasis. The leader swerved sharply to the left and the other dogs followed, sending up a cloud of powdered snow.

The low, uneven horizon of the east was ruddy with the Arctic dawn. Behind us the moon and stars faded in the red light; before us arid hills remained dark in a haze of dull light; in the sky small clouds floated in a radiant crimson glow.

Minute by minute, as we sped along, the darkness ahead retreated; the pale blue of the sky gradually became more glorious. But on the white ground of the earth there was only an austere uniformity of dim light, forming no shadow. Thus the day dawned, clear and cold.

"*Auk—auk!*" grunted Utik.

The guttural command for a turn to the right came

RIDING THE TEMPEST

with throat-tearing sharpness. Our leader obeyed instantly. We sped out over the frozen surface of a lagoon that extended for miles in the direction we were going. Now that we had left the uneven ground behind us, our speed increased perceptibly. The sledge was light and the going good, so Utik jumped on.

Several times in succession Utik called *"Huit!"* with a peculiar trill in his voice. The dogs broke from a run into a gallop. From their quick breathing a hazy vapour enveloped them, and as they raced ahead, wisps of it trailed to the rear. Through it I could see the dogs, their bushy tails swaying in unison from side to side, as their shaggy backs moved under the powerful down-thrust of arching legs.

The sledge runners creaked and scraped on the frozen surface and, bumping over small lumps of ice, fell with a hollow, ringing sound. These sounds were reproduced by the ice-covered lagoon, which gave off a dull, continued resonance.

It was an exhilarating ride, although the wind bit at my exposed face until the tears came and I had to knock my feet together to keep the blood moving. From time to time Utik clapped his hands together; whether it was to keep them warm or to encourage the dogs was more than I could make out.

The rapid pace at which we were travelling soon brought us to the farther reach of the lagoon. The bank was steep and we alighted to assist the dogs in getting over the obstacle.

"*Huit !*" yelled Utik.

The dogs sped across the ice and started up the ridge, but before they reached the top, the sledge came to rest, canted at an angle of forty-five degrees. To give the dogs a breathing spell, Utik unlashed the bridle and disentangled the traces. When he had everything ready, he motioned for me to stand at the rear of the sledge and push when he gave the word.

Stationing himself near the front of the sledge, Utik took hold of the bridle with both hands. Setting himself by digging his heels in the snow, he pulled sideways until all of the slack on the traces was taken up.

"*Huit !*" he cried.

At the same time he let go of the bridle and gave a smart kick to the runner of the sledge with his foot, while I shoved for all I was worth. At the word, the dogs leaped forward to the length of their traces, and with arched legs began clawing their way up the bank. Their gallant effort carried them to the crest and on over. The other sledge, following in our wake, had easier going ; and we went on without a pause.

Toward midday we halted near a small brook. Utik cut a hole in the ice while his companion turned the sledges upside down, preparatory to re-icing the mud shoeings of the runners. As soon as the job was

RIDING THE TEMPEST

finished, we started again on our way without bothering to eat, it being customary to stop only for necessities when a destination was to be reached by nightfall, and good did not come in the class of necessities.

By mid-afternoon the ride did not appear so pleasant to me. I was hungry and cold. The sun had gradually commenced its slide down towards the distant hills and the temperature was dropping with it. I tried running alongside of the sledge to keep warm, but so good was the road and so rapid the pace of the dogs that, running at top speed, I was unable to keep up. I resumed my place in the sledge with a painful feeling of chill in my body.

The trail passed through an expanse of willows where the snow was deep and soft. In this the dogs sank to their bellies and even then they could not find a solid bottom to grip with their paws. The sledges sank in and dragged heavily.

I was glad of the chance to work the chill out of my body. The combined efforts of men and dogs worked the sledges forward foot by foot. Frequently the dogs disappeared under the clouds of snow they raised in their effort to get a solid footing. The whips bit and stung.

There was a medley of shouts from the drivers. "*Harra!—Auk!—Huit!*" ("Go to the left!—Turn to the right!—Go ahead!") It was bewildering. Man and dogs were panting; but none stopped exerting themselves, and the wooden handles of the whips rose and fell on the dogs.

In the confusion, getting hard blows which they did not deserve, the dogs of Utik's team turned upon each other and, in spite of yells, commands, and the bite of the whip, they kept tearing at each other until they were exhausted. Finally the fight ceased and the yelps of pain of the bitten dogs began. During the whole performance, not one of the animals had turned on its human tormentors, so deeply is the fear of man imprinted in them.

It was useless to work the dogs further, so they were unharnessed and tied apart, while Utik and the "White Man" pulled in the harness and I shoved from behind. As Utik's team had trampled and packed the snow, the "White Man" had no trouble in getting through with his dogs, and the drive was resumed on the firm snow as though nothing had happened.

The dogs were tired and that cut our speed. So we decided to make camp on the shore of a river not far from the coast, a spot some three or four hours distant.

To a pallid horizon, where the setting sun was now flinging flaming rays through breaks in accumulating clouds, the wilderness extended its bleak whiteness. A storm was brewing. From afar the winds began to howl eerily, while the distant reports of cracking ice added a deep, muffled undertone.

RIDING THE TEMPEST

I felt miserable. My exertions had soaked me with perspiration and the bitter cold bit through to the marrow of my bones. The blasts of the coming storm, too, filled me with a sense of oppression. I tried to run alongside the *komutik*, but it was no use. It was too much for me and I resumed by place on the sledge.

A vague torpor took hold of me, and with its coming the keen sensation of pain that gnawed at me departed. Snow, borne by the shrieking wind, lashed my face; I was aware of the deep night, the snow, the jolts of the sledge; but I felt no pain. At intervals I heard the voice of Utik as he called to the huskies.

We came to the crest of the bluff that commanded the river at the place where we intended to camp. The way down was steep and slippery, but Utik did not slow down. He slipped a corded walrus thong under the runners as a brake and sent the dogs down at a full gallop.

The incline suddenly became steeper. The dogs, unable to stop, dug in their claws, leaving streaks of blood in the snow. Utik threw himself down beside the sledge in an effort to control its pace, but despite him the sledge swept ahead of the dogs before they were half-way down. Yelping and howling, the huskies were dragged along by the runaway *komutik*, while I crouched on the careering sledge.

For the moment I was powerless to move. The sledge swayed from its course. A huge boulder, towering threateningly, loomed ahead. Utik gave a mighty shove to the right. The sledge went as directed. The dogs, unable to control themselves, went to the other side.

Crack! The traces broke. The dogs, released by the broken lines, rolled pell-mell down the slope. The sledge slithered in toward the rock, tilted, upset and rolled to the bottom of the incline, with Utik and myself following in its wake.

Utik picked himself up and looked over his sledge. It had a broken runner. The other team had topped the crest and was following in our wake. The "White Man" had better luck, and as he passed us, Utik shouted to attract his attention; having reached the bottom, he retraced his way to where we awaited him.

The "White Man" got the dogs together, and we transferred my belongings to his *komutik*, placing the broken sledge on top of the load, and made our way down to the river flats. An igloo was put up and a warm supper was eaten.

After feeding the dogs, Utik went down to the river bank. He was concerned because the river, which was very swift at that spot, was not entirely frozen over. He wanted to turn back, and the "White Man" felt the same way. So it was decided.

In the igloo we went to sleep, while the wail of the rising storm came faintly to our ears, muffled by the wall of ice that shielded us from its wrath.

CHAPTER V

I WAS A FRENCHMAN. I BECOME AN ESKIMO

IT took us two days to get back to the post. The sun had disappeared when the buildings came into sight, and it was the howling of the dogs that announced our return. From the scattered igloos the no-good "White Men" came running. The door of the bunkhouse opened and Thevenet stood outlined against the glow that streamed out across the snow.

"Hallo!" he shouted.

"Hallo!" I answered back.

Utik swung the team in a wide circle and pulled up at the entrance. I threw off the robes that covered me and stood up, stamping my feet to get my blood into circulation. It was warm and cozy in the shack.

"You are back soon, *mon enfant*," said Thevenet, who had followed me inside. "Something has happened, eh?"

I nodded briefly.

"Then you did not get to the village?" asked Drollet, rubbing his nose with the back of his hand.

"No," I answered, and I told them of the accident and of our decision to return.

KABLUK OF THE ESKIMO

But while I was talking, Ahoyak, our Eskimo servant, came in, bringing a pot of steaming beans and bear meat; she went to the cupboard and brought back a plate, which she rubbed with the sleeve of her dirty blouse, and placed it before me with a knife and fork. I was hungry and I began to eat.

Things at "The Fort" remained the same and I fell into the old routine. In the morning we did the chores, fixing things up and looking after the dogs; in the afternoon we went partridge-hunting to pass the time; in the evening we sat together sociably before a roaring fire; and by eleven o'clock we were abed.

With the first signs of spring the Indians came. A small party of Naskopies, a tribe that live in the interior of Labrador, arrived at "The Fort" and stayed in the neighbourhood for a short time.

The Indians were tall, fine-looking men, with long, arched noses, beautiful eyes, and wonderful teeth. When talking to you, they looked you straight in the eye, but I soon found out that in spite of their fine appearance they were not to be trusted. It was amazing how things disappeared before we got wise to their ways.

I soon discovered that the Indians and the Eskimos did not get along together at all. Even the "White Men", worthless as they were, would have nothing to do with the red men. The Naskopies regarded the Eskimos as dirty beasts, too filthy to be seen with; and the Eskimo viewpoint was epitomized by Utik.

I BECOME AN ESKIMO

"Indian, faugh!" he said, holding his nose. "Much caribou dung."

The Naskopies camped on one side of "The Fort" in their wigwams made of tanned deerskins, and the Eskimos stayed on the other side in their tents. It was soon evident that we would have to have separate trading rooms for both in order to avoid trouble, so we arranged two wickets for that purpose.

With the coming of the Indians, the fur-trading season started. We traded for the fox pelts they brought, and after they had departed the Eskimo tribes began to come around. They would stay for a short time and move on, while other families would come along to take their place. The Indians came only at infrequent intervals, bringing beaver, fox, and otter pelts mostly.

That first season at "The Fort" we did not do much business. Most of the Eskimos came to look over the place of the "*Oui, oui, mao*", as they called us; but they did their trading with Duncan Mathison, the factor at the Hudson Bay Company post, who treated them strictly but fairly, and as a result exercised a tremendous power over them.

I was busy looking over a bundle of marten pelts when a shadow fell athwart the counter. A patriarchal Eskimo stood before me, aloof but friendly. It was Akpek, the chief.

"*Chimo*," he rumbled, and was silent.

"*Chimo*," I answered, and waited for him to speak again.

The chief's eyes wandered over the shelves stocked with goods for barter and around the bins where the furs were to be stored, the while making a soft clucking noise that came from deep within his barrel-like chest.

"You come with empty hands," I said finally, throwing the skins into a bin.

"Aha, yes."

"And why is that?"

"For long my people have traded with 'The men on that side'."

"Then why come you here?"

"To see you, my son," he said simply. "Akpek and Nayume have thought much of you."

"Aha; and I of you and 'armarruluk'. How is the little girl?"

"Well," he said, adding, "The trail at the river is bad."

"You have heard of my journey?"

"Aha!" said the patriarch gravely. "In the North, word is spread by the winds, and the snows whisper to us its secrets."

"That is so," I said, nodding.

"You have been good to Akpek," he continued, "and I am here."

"Aha, yes."

I BECOME AN ESKIMO

"The Eskimo does not forget."

Akpek turned and stalked toward the door. At the threshold he paused.

"You will visit Akpek's tent to-night?" he queried.

"Aha, yes."

The tent of Akpek stood alone at some distance from the post. It was late when I started; but the sun was still above the horizon, and a glorious moon shed a mysterious glow over the Arctic landscape. The barking of the dogs brought Akpek to the entrance of his dwelling.

I followed him into the tent. At one side Nayume, his woman, sat sewing a garment of caribou hide; beside her, on a pallet of deerskins, the young girl, Amaluke, was sleeping peacefully.

"Our daughter is well," said Nayume, noticing my glance. She motioned me to a pile of pelts, and I sat down. Akpek bobbed his grey old head in assent.

"That is good," I said.

For a while there was silence. Nayume stitched busily away at her *shelepak*, the frock worn by full-grown women. Akpek sat motionless, puffing slowly at his stone pipe. I watched the nimble fingers of Nayume and marvelled at their skill.

"It will soon be the season for the *ai'vuk*, the great tusked walrus, my son," rumbled Akpek.

"Aha."

The patriarch exhaled a cloud of smoke, belching it

out in a single gigantic puff. It vanished upward, revealing his weather-carved features. Outside there was a sudden growling among the dogs that died abruptly away.

"You will come with us for the hunt?" the patriarch grunted.

"*Emarha*—maybe."

Again Akpek filled his lungs with smoke and emitted it with a single exhalation. Nayume finished her work and set it aside. I knocked the ashes from my pipe and arose.

"When do you leave for the hunt?"

"So many sleeps," Akpek answered, holding up his ten fingers.

"Good," I responded. "*Chimo.*"

"*Chimo.*"

The next morning I talked the matter over with my companions. There was little to do at the post, and it was excellent business to get in the good graces of the tribe of which Akpek was the chief. The hunt would give me a chance to gain their respect and goodwill, and so it was decided I should go.

Akpek had come to the post with several families of his tribe by kayak. The silver fox were abundant and Akpek and his people brought many of them. I eyed the glistening sheen of the furs with infinite pleasure, and promised myself that I would learn the country whence the beauties came. In the early part

Courtesy G. Herodier

"WHEN DO YOU LEAVE FOR THE HUNT?"
"SO MANY SLEEPS," AKPEK ANSWERED, HOLDING UP HIS TEN FINGERS

I BECOME AN ESKIMO

of June—or, as the Eskimo calendar runs, "When the caribou have calves"—we left for his village. I was to ride with the chief in his kayak.

I had seen the native craft, but never at close range, and when we assembled at the river I wondered where I was to ride. Akpek's kayak was some eighteen feet in length; amidships where the paddler sat in a sort of well, it was two feet across. Its shape tapered at both ends; the bow was pointed and had a pronounced upturn, while the stern was as sharp, but slightly less bent. It was covered with sealskin.

"*Allons, mon enfant*," cried Thevenet jovially. "And where do you ride? Or are you going to handle it yourself, eh?"

The chief pointed to the back of the kayak. I gathered that he was expecting me to lie face down at the back of the craft. I took my place with a certain trepidation, holding myself flat and motionless. Akpek took his place and with a shove of his broad-bladed paddle sent the kayak out into the stream.

The river was at the flood and we swept downstream at a rapid rate of speed. Gradually, in spite of myself, my tired, cramped muscles relaxed; my body followed the balancing motion of the kayak without trouble. I found it a very comfortable way to ride and there was no danger at all of being rolled overboard.

With only an inch or two of freeboard astern, the kayak moved forward buoyantly and swiftly. Once or twice a swirl of water threatened to swamp the craft; but each time it rose easily, without being touched by the flying spray.

Watching Akpek as he wielded his double paddle with a light, swaying motion from left to right, I thought of the centaur, the fabulous man-horse of mythology. Every movement of the paddler was reflected in his craft, the bow moving with a rhythmic left and right sway, under the impulse of his stroke.

Resting my head upon the crook of my arm, I watched the swirling waters pass in close proximity to my face. At times, hiding the river bank from view, huge chunks of ice would slide by and disappear rearward.

The musical murmuring of the waters made me drowsy and I went to sleep. I was awakened by voices. The party had reached the mouth of the Koksoak, and we were to camp there for the night. I slept well.

Next morning we ate hurriedly to catch the ebb tide, which would be helpful in carrying us northward. The party made good progress and the sun was low on the horizon when, doubling around a headland, we came into sight of the Iglulik village.

I raised myself on my forearms and, gazing over the shoulder of Akpek, I stared intently at the dark line of sealskin tents that stood out against the pale sky in irregular and broken outlines.

The men, women and children of the village

I BECOME AN ESKIMO

thronged the shore, quiet, but with happy grins at the safe return of the chief and his party. The dogs yelped merrily. The kayaks, led by the chief, raced for the shore. As they touched the strand, the men of the village hastened to help bring them ashore.

Once on land the ceremony of introduction began. The shaman of the tribe came first. He stepped forward, placing himself right in front of me.

"I am Tickek. I mean no evil. I have no knife to be feared. Who are you?"

It was evident that he was introducing himself, but as my knowledge of the language did not enable me to understand thoroughly, I merely smiled, saying, "White man." The medicine man stared at me steadily for a few moments longer, and saying, "Kablunark," turned away.

The introductions went on apace, each repeating the formula given by the shaman, while I simply smiled and said, "White man," over and over again.

A little boy, unable to say the longer word, shortened my Eskimo title to "Kabluk", and everybody laughed. The nickname, as nicknames often do, stuck; and from that time on I was known as Kabluk.

Thus was "Kabluk of the Eskimo" born.

There was something in that primeval huddle of savage habitations that affected me profoundly. The bleak immensity that hedged it in struck a responsive chord in my breast and I felt that I was returning home.

KABLUK OF THE ESKIMO

For the first time I felt the iron grip that held my heart loosen. At last I was home. Home!

Akpek's tent was large and the ground was covered with mats of caribou skin. We ate in silence and went to bed.

CHAPTER VI

THEY OFFER ME NORRAK, THE BLONDE GIRL OF THE TRIBE

IT was broad daylight when the family of Akpek, the chief, began to stir. I awoke much refreshed. My surroundings were a bit strange, but there was something soothing in that rough habitation, something homelike and familiar, that made me feel at peace with the world.

Nayume was preparing breakfast outside; and the old man, seated near her, was passively smoking his stone pipe. Through the open flap of the tent I could see a segment of dull sky and at intervals men, women, children and the dogs of the village roamed back and forth. Many fires were sending pillars of smoke up into the heavens.

As I stared, a shadow darkened the opening, and Nayume entered, bearing a steaming stone kettle of savoury meat. Akpek followed at her heels and seated himself near me. Placing the stone pot between us, she called to me.

Eskimo women do not eat with their lords; they wait on them and, when their masters' appetites are satisfied, they dine on what is left. In turn, the dogs wait patiently in front of the opening for scraps and bones; and, the women having eaten, the dogs get the rest.

Amaluke, the little girl, still slept, and Nayume shook her. There was something vaguely familiar in the domestic scene. It brought back memories of my mother. Nayume went about her duties in stolid but efficient manner. After the meal I went to the bank of a small pond near by where I washed my face and arms.

The chief's wife was a tall woman of simple demeanour, with bright eyes and clean-cut features. She still possessed indications of the haunting beauty of her youthful days. The *shelepak* she wore had a short flap descending to her knees in front and a longer one in the rear; the hood of the garment was large and finished with long fringes. Underneath she wore trousers, baggy at the knees, which gave her legs a queer appearance. Her costume throughout was fancifully trimmed with furs of contrasting colours and bone ornaments.

The village consisted of some twenty tents, identical in shape with that of Akpek, but of varying dimensions. Each family had pitched its tent in a favourable spot, without considering the layout of the village as a whole.

The place at first appeared untidy and unwholesome, but I saw at once that there was no germ-breeding refuse among the rubbish that cluttered the village.

THEY OFFER ME NORRAK

Everything eatable that was thrown out was snapped up greedily by the dogs and the bones were gnawed clean.

On high racks flesh of walrus, seals, and caribou was drying in the sun; hides and furs, too, were placed high above the ground to keep them from the dogs. Over all hung an odour that was unpleasant to my uneducated nostrils, but it was not in the least offensive, and in time it passed without notice.

I took a seat upon a rock that rested on the hillside, a point from where I could observe the animated activities of the little colony.

Boys were playing in the open spaces; shooting arrows at a mark, cracking long whips, throwing the trout spear, and earnestly wrestling. The more mature were helping their parents in their various tasks.

Among the men various works were in progress. Most of them were at work on their *komutiks*, others were busy repairing kayaks on the shore, and the rest were seated before their various dwellings, carving implements for the household or the hunt from ivory, stone, or wood.

Busiest of all were the women. Walking to and fro, young mothers chanted guttural melodies to quiet, naked babies carried in large hoods on their backs. Coming from the shore, a group of women, half concealed under enormous loads of driftwood, carried on an animated chattering in spite of their heavy burdens;

and from the frequent bursts of laughter as they passed I gathered that they were making fun of me, "Kabluk of the Eskimo".

I left my perch and followed them at a distance. Before the tent of Tickek, the *angekok*, a woman was busily scraping fat from a hide; beside her another was stretching a skin on a wide drying-frame of willow. Further on I passed an old woman squatted before a cauldron hung from a tripod over a low fire, stirring a thick yellowish concoction of an oily nature. Near by a young girl sat, cracking bones with a stone, taking care not to crush them, so that the precious marrow could be extracted whole.

I continued on down to a little cove where the watercraft were assembled. The boats were all drawn up on the shore. A man was at work on one of the kayaks, and I drew nearer. The man, who answered to the name of Anotinoak, smiled at my interest, being glad to find someone who appreciated his ability as a craftsman.

From the Eskimo's mouth two canine teeth, one on each side, projected like a short pair of tusks, giving him a rather striking resemblance to a young walrus. Together with the tattooed lines on his chin, they added as much to Anotinoak's reputation for good looks as the attention I was bestowing upon his handicraft added to his prominence in the village.

At close quarters I noticed a peculiar odour

Courtesy National Museum of Canada

BUSIEST OF ALL WERE THE WOMEN
MRS. AURORA BOREALIS CHEWING SEALSKIN FOR MR. AURORA BOREALIS' BOOTS

THEY OFFER ME NORRAK

emanating from Anotinoak, the Eskimo scent, but I was becoming used to it. When I got to the windward of him, I noticed that he wrinkled his nose and moved away. At first I did not sense anything wrong, but when it happened again and again, I was dumbfounded to realize that my aroma, the white-man smell, was as disagreeable to him as his had originally been to me.

Nevertheless, Anotinoak did all that he could to put me at my ease. I examined the kayak carefully. The frame was built up from driftwood, two long sticks forming the rails to which the light ribs are securely lashed.

Among the smaller vessels there were several queer-looking skin boats about twenty feet long; in shape they resembled a long, wide box, flaring out along the sides; and for their size they were extremely light. They were propelled by oars and sail.

Using the few words I knew, supplemented by signs, I asked Anotinoak what they were. With expressive features and a rapid flow of language, he tried to enlighten me. Seeing that I did not grasp his meaning he pointed to the boat, saying "*Umeak*"; and then turning to where a group of women were at work, he said "*Arnak*", making it obvious that the craft was used by the women.

The sun was setting behind the rocky top of the island when I left my Eskimo friend. Retracing my way to the abode of Akpek I met many of the villagers. All looked at me with a curiosity they politely tried to hide, and all greeted me with a good-natured grin.

I found Nayume waiting for the men under her care to arrive. Akpek was already there, patiently listening to Amaluke, as though she were a grown woman, while she mothered her wooden doll. Calling the child to her, Nayume placed a kettle of hot soup, made of caribou blood, before us. It was a dish that Akpek relished and to me it was not unappetizing.

With the coming of dawn on the day after my arrival, the first scouting party went out to seek for *ai'vuk*, the walrus. The days went quickly by. Everyone was busy in anticipation of the coming hunt.

I spent much of my time in the tent of Akpek. He was, I found, of a melancholy disposition, silent and meditative, meaning well by his dependants and the people he led. Nayume, motherly and inquisitive, assumed the burden of instructing me in the Eskimo tongue. Seated in the tent, stitching away at a *shelepak*, Nayume began tutoring me in the language of her people, explaining mostly by signs; and little Amaluke laughed heartily at the ludicrousness of some of my replies.

From Nayume I learned nearly every word of the Eskimo language, one by one; curiosity and a good memory on my side, and patience and good humour on hers, produced rapid results.

THEY OFFER ME NORRAK

The guttural pronunciation was difficult for me to acquire at first, and little Amaluke laughed heartily whenever an accent, wrongly placed, produced a word of different meaning to the one I had in mind. Not so with her elders. My desire to learn the language flattered them, and they took pains to assist me.

The words, I discovered, were inflected as regularly as in ancient Greek. The language, too, was much richer than French in words that pertained to their daily activities : hunting, fishing, and animal life.

I roamed over the island. It was a solid mass of weather-stained rocks and boulders, with hollows and crevices in which rain and snow-water gathered. Of trees or willows in its confines there were none. Quantities of driftwood, however, paralleled the shore, the high tides each season adding to the debris.

To the east of the island lay the open sea ; in the south and west a large channel separated it from the mainland ; and many islands were to be seen scattered over the ocean to the north. In the same direction, when the light was favourable, I discerned the outline of a distant land.

Life among the simple beings with whom I was staying appealed to me. In that remote part of the world I lived a far happier existence than might seem possible. I had nothing to worry about. The Eskimo had no clocks, no calendars, no money. The men hunted and fished that the tribe might eat ; each night,

KABLUK OF THE ESKIMO

tired with their labour in the open, invigorating air of the North, came dreamless sleep.

Under the myriads of icy-pointed stars I would seat myself upon the sandy shore, where the expiring breath of the land breeze fluttered with the warmth of the last fine days of summer. At such times a deathlike silence pervaded the earth, the sky, the sea; and it penetrated my whole being with its mournful significance.

The days passed into weeks and still there was no sign of *ai'vuk*, the walrus. But I never found life monotonous. There was always a new bit of knowledge to absorb, some useful work to do, some genuine fun to be had. I listened to the legends and strange stories told by the elders, gaining an insight into the history of the northland and its people; and the peculiar songs and music gave me a deep abiding pleasure.

Now that I could converse with the villagers, I made it a point to visit them regularly, going to every tent in turn. From this personal contact and by constantly talking with the people, I gained considerable knowledge of their character, ability, and disposition.

I did not allow myself to be influenced by petty quarrels and jealousies in forming my estimates of the villagers. The Eskimos were as human and as subject to weaknesses as civilized people are, but in their case the pettiness and peculiarities were the result of their primitive appetites and superstitious beliefs, which they were unable to control.

THEY OFFER ME NORRAK

"Why have you two wives?" I asked Anotinoak one day.

"Because I can look after them," he explained, proud of being able to give proof of his ability as a craftsman and a clever hunter. Then, taking my question as a hint that I had no woman, while he had two, he pointed to the youngest, and said:

"You can have this one."

"I thank my friend for his offer," I told him, "but I do not want a woman. White men may marry but one wife. Why may the Eskimo have more than one?"

"Amongst my people there are more women than men. If each man was to take one wife, what would the other women do? Who would feed them? Who would clothe them? Who would defend them? How could they bear children without a mate?

"Women need men as much as men need women. The good hunter can provide more food than he can use: why not let him share it with as big a family as he can feed? Besides, a good hunter has more hides to dry, more furs to stretch; he uses more boots and clothes, consequently needing more women to make new ones."

The old boatbuilder's reasoning was forceful enough, as I had to admit. Pondering over the matter, I concluded that the Eskimo was neither moral nor immoral; he was simply governed by the conditions of his

KABLUK OF THE ESKIMO

everyday life and, in the full meaning of the phrase, he lived naturally.

For some time the fifteen-year-old daughter of Anguti had dressed in the costume affected by marriageable young women; but she did not find approval among the unmarried men, although she was a girl of many accomplishments. I wondered at it.

Norrak's eyes were dark grey; her red lips always wore an engaging smile; and she had a shyness of manner that struck me as singularly attractive. The most remarkable feature of Norrak was her auburn hair. It blazoned to the world her mixed descent and called to mind the arrival of a whaler on business bound—and pleasure.

In the eyes of her people she was ugly; the only feature that she possessed that appealed to them was her feet, which turned slightly inward when she walked, as those belonging to good-looking girls were expected to do. Her mother often sighed: "What a pity she is so unsightly!" and she worried over having given birth to such an abnormal child.

I found her company delightful; and, contrary to local etiquette, I made it a practice to accompany her on her expeditions in search of edible plants and berries. Norrak taught me how to recognize the varieties of medicinal plants employed by her people, and explained their uses.

It was not long before I found that my company

THEY OFFER ME NORRAK

was not unattractive to her. She put herself in my path and I spent much time with her. I suddenly became aware of a desire to kiss my companion, whose appearance was so different from that of the other Eskimo girls.

But kissing is unknown among the Eskimos. The customary method of expressing affection or tenderness is to place the nose against the cheek of the person to be greeted and sniff deeply. It is a method seldom used among the adults.

The villagers began to look knowingly at each other when we appeared. That they expected me to take Norrak as my mate was soon evident. It was not to be thought of, however, and I gave up my delightful rambles over the island, spending the day in silent communing with Akpek in his tent.

One day I was resting after the evening meal, when guests, a woman and her little boy, arrived. I sat on the woven mats playing with Amaluke and the lad, when the woman, wishing him to throw a bone to the dogs, spoke to him.

"If your daughter asked you to throw this bone to the dogs, would my little father go?" she asked, addressing the boy with the deference due to an adult as is the custom.

"No, I wouldn't!" whined the child in a sulky tone, angry at being disturbed.

"But daughter would be so pleased if her little

KABLUK OF THE ESKIMO

father would do it," the mother begged in a respectful tone, in which not a shade of annoyance or anger could be detected.

"No."

"Is my little father very sure he will not do that for me?" she cooed, patting him in a gentle manner.

"I won't," screamed the child in a temper, kicking furiously at his mother. "No! No! I won't!"

The ill-natured lad stopped of his own accord only when his howls and struggles had exhausted his strength, while his mother continued to pet him. After they had gone, I turned to Akpek for an explanation of what I had just seen.

"That woman's father died four years ago," explained the chief, "shortly before the child was born. His body was buried on the hill; but his soul fluttered expectantly around the tent where she lay, waiting to enter the body of the baby that was about to come to life.

"During the three days that followed the birth of the child, the mother gently and persistently invited her father's spirit to take up his abode in the infant, so that the child could acquire his wisdom. At last her pleading was heard, her prayers gratified, so the shaman announced.

"The woman is really dealing with her father's soul, and she must treat it with the proper respect; so whatever the boy wants to do, his mother must permit without question."

Courtesy National Museum of Canada

THE WOMAN IS REALLY DEALING WITH HER FATHER'S SOUL
—SO WHATEVER THE BOY WANTS TO DO HIS MOTHER MUST
PERMIT

THEY OFFER ME NORRAK

Six weeks passed. The scouts were still unable to locate the wary *ai'vuk*. I was due back at the post before the salmon run commenced early in August, and I spoke to Akpek.

"It is now the time of the mosquito," I said, "and the walrus has not come."

"Aha, yes."

"They will not come?"

"*Ai'vuk* is late this year."

"I must return to my people."

"The tent of Akpek will be empty."

"The heart of Kabluk will be empty too."

"Aha!" said the chief sadly.

"But I will come again."

"That is good."

The villagers rose early to witness my departure. The chief had assigned Uyarak, his nephew, to escort me back to the post. On the beach the entire population stood in silence, except for the yelping of the dogs. As we rounded the promontory I looked back and waved my arm in farewell. But the villagers were already going about their daily tasks. A single figure still gazed seaward. Akpek's upraised arm sped me on my way.

CHAPTER VII

A YEAR ALONE ON LOON ISLAND

TOWARD the end of August the steamer *Stord* came again up the Koksoak River. I stood on the bank while Yvon Drollet, the factor, went aboard to talk with the captain in his cabin. In a short time he came on deck and shouted for me to come aboard. He introduced me to the captain, a swarthy-faced French-Canadian.

"The captain has brought a message for you," said Drollet, and he handed me a sheet of paper bearing the mark of Revillon Frères. I read it slowly.

I was ordered to report at company headquarters in Montreal, preparatory to going to Cape Dufferin, on the west coast of Labrador, to open a new post. I looked up with a wrinkled brow.

"It is a feather in your cap, *mon ami,*" cried Drollet enthusiastically. "Soon you will be a factor with a post of your own."

I could not see it that way, but I said nothing. I got my stuff together and took it aboard. The season had been a bad one and it did not take long to load the furs on the boat. We shoved off, and with an ache

ALONE ON LOON ISLAND

in my heart, I saw the post disappear. I was homesick.

It seemed to me that I had never before seen such a populous place as that famous old French-Canadian city. Everywhere you turned there were people, and everything was cramped and stuffy: the streets, the dwellings, the churches, and the warehouses. That place did not seem like home to me.

The shrieking whistles of the boats on the river and from the factories tore at my eardrums, giving me a headache; and even the church bells sounded loud and clangorous. Worst of all was the continuous roar of traffic, the old horse traffic of years ago, and the shouts of newsboys and vendors. It all bewildered me, and I thought with longing of the quiet and peace of Akpek's village.

As I walked through the streets, I was pushed and jostled by the passers-by, who hurried on their way without giving me even a single thought, and I was overcome with an intense loneliness.

The thoroughfares were crowded with vehicles of all kinds. In a hurrying stream they passed: trucks, drays, and fine carriages. Their drivers shouted to me to get out of their way. *Sacré Dieu!* I thought they would run me down. Leaving the main street, I went to my destination by a roundabout route.

A man had been sent to Cape Dufferin and it was with infinite relief I learned that I was to be sent into the North immediately on another job. I felt that to remain in the city for any length of time would make me as mad as an Arctic wolf.

"Since I am not to go to Cape Dufferin," I asked the official, "where am I to go?"

"Loon Island," said the clerk. "One of our boats, the *El Dorado*, went on the rocks there. She has a valuable cargo aboard, and if we leave it unprotected over the winter we will never see it again."

He paused to scribble on a sheet of paper and then went on: "It will have to be guarded until the break-up of the ice next year will permit salvaging. That is your job."

As I still remained silent, he looked up: "You understand your instructions?"

"Perfectly," I said briefly.

"Good," he answered, cramming some papers in an envelope, which he left unsealed and handed to me. "You will go by rail to Missanabie. It is the jumping-off place for those bound overland to Moose Factory. Get some Indian guides there and you will be all right."

On the train I studied the map in the time-table. I located Missanabie. To the north, on the lower end of James Bay, three hundred and fifty miles away, was Moose Factory; not far as distances go in the Northland, but a long jump for one who had no experience with snowshoes. And I had never had a snowshoe on before.

ALONE ON LOON ISLAND

At Missanabie I hired my guides and we started. My party consisted of an old Indian called Stephen, and two young bucks. They used the Cree snowshoe, narrow and long, and excellent for going in loose snow. I was using snowshoes I had got from the Indians at "The Fort"; they were broad and flat, tapering at the rear, and were fine for rolling country where the snow was hard packed.

From the very start things went wrong. Like the greenhorn I was, I started the trek with too much grub. We were travelling through a game country and there was plenty of fresh meat to be had. Had we travelled light we would have made excellent time, but pulling the three toboggans, heavily loaded, cut our speed proportionately.

We had not gone far when we hit the snow country. The fall had been exceptionally heavy that year and it was very deep and soft. At first we took turns in beating the trail; but my snowshoes were so wide, they did not help me at all. It was terrible. The snow was so yielding that even with the snowshoes I would sink in a foot. The Indians had an easier time of it.

I was a strong fellow, but the grind was too much for me. My feet were soon covered with blisters and I could hardly walk. The Indians knew that I was green, and they kept asking for more grub. Not knowing any better, I let them fill their bellies and our supply began to dwindle.

KABLUK OF THE ESKIMO

At Long Portage we came across the fresh tracks of a herd of moose. My feet needed a rest, and the fresh meat would be very welcome, so I decided to stay over a couple of days. The rest did me good and we went after the moose.

We came up to six of them in an area that had been burned over. I knocked down two of them with my rifle and the rest darted away into the scrub. Running after them, I caught my foot in a fallen tree and sprained it. It hurt like the devil, but we could not stay any longer and we went on.

There was still two hundred miles to go, and in spite of my aches, I had to keep going forward. The snow became worse, the going harder, the food less. Because of my condition, we could travel for only short periods at a time. The Indians were beginning to show the effects of the trip too.

We had to leave one of the toboggans, transferring the remainder of its load to the other two. Things got worse and worse. The game had vanished. My condition became more painful. My nose bled almost constantly, and I began to have light-headed spells.

It looked as though we were done for, unless we got aid. I decided to send the young Indians for help. Stephen, the old Indian, stayed with me. We put all of our belongings on one toboggan, abandoning the other, and limped along in their track, he pulling while I pushed.

ALONE ON LOON ISLAND

When we were about a hundred miles from Moose Factory, we ran out of food altogether. A hundred miles in the North is no distance at all, but we were done in. It was impossible for us to go farther. Stephen understood some English, and I could speak enough words to make him understand what I was talking about.

"Me, you," I said. "Stay here. Make shelter. If we die, we die here."

The old man did not say a word. He began to gather boughs for the shelter. The weather turned colder, and when you have the cold weather on an empty stomach, it is no joke. My ankle had swollen so that I could not walk, and Stephen had to do the work; but he was getting very weak too.

Every night he put out snares. The first two days we did not catch a thing, but on the third Stephen came back to the shelter, bringing a wee little rabbit. Holla! We were hungry. I could hardly wait while Stephen singed the hair from the carcass; and we ate every bit of it, insides and all.

That morsel gave us a new lease of life. My ankle was much better and I decided to hit the trail again. It was better than sitting around and freezing. There was no use in dragging along the empty toboggan that remained, and we abandoned it.

We trudged along through the deep snow all that day and all of the next. We made fairly good time, travelling light as we were. The second night was bad. More cold on an empty belly. On the next morning we reached an Indian camp. We stumbled into it almost half dead.

The Indians did not have much food but they gave us of what they had. They had flour and we stayed there all day, feasting on pancakes—pancakes, dirty and greasy, but I have seldom tasted anything as good.

On the following morning we started on again. My leg was better and we travelled at a good pace. About forty miles from Moose Factory we saw two dog-teams coming toward us.

"There is our relief," I cried, stopping dead in my tracks.

My Indian companion said nothing, and we waited for the dog-teams to come up. The drivers, a French-Canadian and a Cree, were surprised to see us. They were not our relief at all. They were bound inland, and could not stop, but they fed us and gave us enough grub to carry us to the post. From them we learned that our Indians had not shown up at Moose Factory.

Thirty-four days after we left Missanabie we staggered into Moose Factory. It was a trip that ordinarily took from twelve to fifteen days. I stayed at the post for a couple of weeks to recuperate.

While there I met a Norwegian who was an old-timer in the North. He invited me to his cabin. He had a very nice-looking daughter. I liked her very much. Black hair, black eyes, and a fine strong figure.

That first time I just sat and smoked with the old man, but my eyes followed the girl as she flitted around the room, getting dinner ready. There, I thought, is a good girl for a wife. The old man talked at a great rate, and I answered him in brief monosyllables. It was late when I left.

The next day I met the girl on the street, as I was hobbling on my way to the water-front. My leg was still in a bad way but the look of solicitude in her eyes made the limp all the more obvious to anyone who cared to look. She greeted me and we walked to the shore together, where we sat on a piece of driftwood.

"It is bad to use your leg," she said. "You must rest it."

"Yes," I answered, longing to fondle her jet-black hair.

"Why do you not stay inside, then," she queried, "until it is better?"

"Then," I answered boldly, "I would not see you."

"Oho!" she cried, pouting prettily. "Now you are making fun of me."

With that she jumped to her feet and made off. I jumped up also but a twinge of pain made me move more slowly and carefully. As I was hobbling along, I met her father, and he started to tell me of his first trip into the North. He was hardly half through when we came to his cabin.

"Come on in," he invited hospitably.

I did so, with alacrity. For an hour or more he related his interminable tale while I let my eyes wander around the room in search of his daughter. She was not in sight, but from behind a closed door came unmistakable sounds that led me to believe that she was in the bedroom and would not come out. Her actions irritated me and I went away, vowing I would not return.

But the next afternoon I was back again, and I remained for supper. She was her delightful self, solicitous about the condition of my leg, and I began to feel that I was mistaken the day before. Day after day I returned to listen to the old man and look at his daughter, and in between we went for short walks together. I liked her pert ways tremendously, and the day before my departure I told her I wanted to marry her.

"Ask Father," was her only answer to my importunities.

That night after supper she went to her room early. I smoked for a while in silence, and then I said:

"I want to marry your daughter."

"What?" growled my host.

"I want to take your daughter as my wife," I reiterated calmly.

ALONE ON LOON ISLAND

"Oh," said the old man, and he puffed slowly on his pipe.

"Well," I asked finally, "will you give your consent?"

"No," he answered. "I will not."

"Why not?" I asked.

"She is too young," he said, and added, "now."

"When I come back, then," I pressed.

"Maybe," he told me. "When you return—we will see."

And with that understanding I left to make preparations for departure on the morrow.

I left for Fort George in a small schooner. We encountered the ice-pack near Twin Islands. The captain ran into a good harbour to wait for a channel to open. There was little grub aboard, and I went ashore to hunt. There were plenty of ducks and geese, and we separated to make sure of a good bag. Toward evening I returned to the shore.

The ship was gone! A solid mass of ice that extended for miles in every direction explained everything. While I was away the ice had moved, and, to avoid being frozen in, the captain had to run for it. My ankle was still a bit weak and I decided to stay where I was.

I was not worried. I had my revolver and cartridges, and the matter of food was easily taken care of; but with the coming of night mosquitoes nearly drove me frantic. Around my ears they buzzed: hundreds, thousands, millions of them. It was impossible for me to sleep, and I walked continuously, seeking relief. If I paused for but a moment, I could feel their stings all over my body.

With the coming of dawn the insects vanished, and I wondered if it all hadn't been a hellish nightmare. I slept through most of the day. Nightfall brought back my tormentors. After five days, a shift in the ice-pack left a stretch of open water, and the schooner then returned to pick me up.

We put in at Fort George, on the eastern shore of Hudson Bay; and I went on by boat to Loon Island, a bare rock with not a single growing thing on it. My companions left me there to act as a lone watchman for a year. The *El Dorado* had gone on to the rocks at high tide, and the receding waters had left her sitting high and dry. She looked as if she was in good condition, perching there on her pinnacle; but a closer look at her hull showed that she would never sail again; the rocks had gouged out her bottom.

On her deck I found a small load of lumber. I took it ashore and built myself a little shack. It had a stove, a bunk, a shelf for some provisions which I salvaged from the wreck, and that was all. I found plenty of work to do. The *El Dorado* carried a valuable cargo, and I began an inventory of its contents.

The work was interesting, if back-breaking, and I went at it with a will. I was only supposed to act

ALONE ON LOON ISLAND

as watchman, but I took it upon myself to sort out the various items that were worth saving, opening cases and marking them.

I was so engrossed in the work that winter—the cold, iron-bound icy grip of the Arctic—came along and took me unawares. There was little fuel to be had; it was mostly driftwood that floated over from the mainland, and it did not amount to much. The woodwork on the wreck was intact, but my sense of responsibility toward the vessel was so great that I did not even think of chopping it up for firewood; although that was what my superiors expected me to do.

I really suffered that winter. Waking up without a fire when the thermometer is down to forty below zero is no joke, by gar! To get my blood circulating I would run, and then I would head down to the shore in search of driftwood. It was seldom that I would find more than I could carry on my back. To save fuel, I cooked but once a week. Several times I went out to the wreck. It was much too cold to work. I was afraid to stay out in the open too long in that freezing temperature, and I spent most of my time in the cabin, huddled in my blankets.

Mon Dieu! It was lonesome. Day after day dragged by without a sign of a living creature. I sat in the cabin hour after hour, bundled up in my blankets, staring out through the little window at the same bleak landscape. I could see across to the mainland, and I would think, think, think.

The library on the *El Dorado* had been taken away, and the only reading matter I could find aboard was an American magazine—and I could not read English. Looking at it, I would formulate in my mind stories that I thought might be found within its secretive pages.

Months passed, and still I remained with my loneliness. I was always a dreamer, and I whiled away the hours in analysing my feelings, my thoughts, my dreams. There was a grandeur about my misery that gave me courage to hold on, a soul-sustaining something that saved me from going mad.

At times I was amazed at my ability to fight off the fits of dejection that came upon me. Ah! In that vast immensity of icy loneliness, I found how puny I was compared to the immutable forces of implacable Nature.

Many times I thought I was mad; that I was caught in the throes of a stupendous nightmare; that there was no longer Romanet, the fur trader. Everything was nothing.

I was afraid to talk aloud, afraid that such a weak concession to my situation would make me go crazy. But I could not control a cough or a sneeze at times, and the unusual sound startled me out of my dreaming.

ALONE ON LOON ISLAND

Gradually everything merged into a limitless, timeless void, in which I dreamed unceasingly, and the facts of everyday existence took on an unreal air.

Many times I thought of Akpek and his village. It was amazing, the vividness with which the phantoms of my mind paraded before me in my little cabin. Again I rode with Akpek on the back of his kayak; again I lived with him in his tent, learning the Eskimo language from Nayume; again I tramped through the village with the patriarchal chief. I stared at his weather-seamed face again, and it vanished in a cloud of smoke, and when it vanished away, I sat on the boulder on the beach at Moose Factory, with a black-haired minx at my side—and then the piercing pain of cramped muscles would bring me to the matter-of-fact present, and, throwing off my blankets, I would stamp around until the warmth crept back into my icy bones.

Toward the end of winter, I spotted a dog-team coming across the ice from the mainland. At first I could not believe my eyes. What would anybody be doing in that desolate spot where not even an animal would come? Not even a fox.

I strained my eyes at the window, rubbing the frost away with frantic fingers. The day was dull, and it was hard to see clearly. The moving blur disappeared behind the wreck, and when I next saw my visitors they were close in to the shore. It was a small party of Eskimos, with two dog-teams.

KABLUK OF THE ESKIMO

They were bound for Richmond Gulf. I needed a change, some kind of activity. I went with them for a trip—just to break the monotony. For a short time I took time off from my job, abandoned my post as a guard watching over the wreck of the *El Dorado*. We were gone for about a week. While travelling along the tremendous cliffs that hedge in Nastapoka Sound we lost one of the dog-teams and its driver. It happened during the course of a bad snowstorm. On the heights the wind was howling in mad fury; and the *komutik*, caught by a savage gust, was swept into the depths.

There was a drop of eight hundred feet at the spot, and it took us a long time to get down to the tragic remains. The driver had both hips broken. He still breathed when we got there, but died shortly afterwards. The dogs had all been killed, and the sledge was kindling wood.

After the accident we returned to Loon Island, and the Eskimo party went on to their village. The sun had returned and I went to work again, salvaging stuff from the wreck. As the sun rose higher, so did my spirits.

The ice went out and the steamer came. We worked like hell putting aboard the stuff I had made ready; and then we started back to Moose Factory.

When we docked at Moose Factory my eyes eagerly scanned the crowd for sight of the face that had filled

ALONE ON LOON ISLAND

my dreams for so many months. She was standing off to one side with her father. She waved to me, and I waved wildly back.

We said little, but our eyes spoke for our tongues. After dinner that night I again broached the subject of marriage to her father, but the old man merely said gruffly:

"She is still too young to know her own mind."

I had to leave, and his word was final. But before I left, my sweetheart and I pledged ourselves to each other, and when I started away, she wept.

CHAPTER VIII

AI'VUK THE WALRUS

AT Montreal my stay at Loon Island was regarded as nothing short of miraculous. The officials crowded around to hear my story, but I had little to say. I answered their questions as best I could, and begged them in time to send me into the North again.

"Where do you wish to go, *mon ami*?" asked the big boss.

The answer was written in my heart, but I meditated silently before answering. "To 'The Fort', " I said.

" 'The Fort'?" said the official. "Where is that?"

"The post on the Koksoak River, sir," supplied a clerk in the room. "It is at the bottom of Ungava Bay."

"So you wish to go back to Ungava, eh?" the big, important personage queried, smiling.

"Yes," I answered.

The clerk whispered in the great man's ear, and he nodded understandingly, staring at me the while. I fidgeted in embarrassment under his quizzical gaze. Picking up a pen, he wrote steadily for some time.

"You will go north on the *Stord* when she sails,"

AI'VUK THE WALRUS

he said, blotting the paper he had written on. A great joy filled my heart, and I tried to express my gratitude, but he motioned for me to be silent. He inserted the folded paper in an envelope and looked up.

"You will deliver these orders to Drollet, your old boss, at Ungava," he said, handing me the letter. "That is all."

The clerk followed me from the room. "Do you know what is in that letter?" he asked, smiling.

I shook my head.

"It is an order telling Drollet that you are to take his place as factor at 'The Fort'."

"What?" I exclaimed. "You are fooling."

"Not at all," he said. "The envelope is open. Read it for yourself."

It was in July 1907 that I again embarked on the steamer *Stord*, bound for Ungava. It was in that part of the world that I had first learned goodness of heart; there I had found peace and contentment. I was going home, and I was happy. The trip was uneventful.

Conditions at "The Fort" had changed much since I had left. The vast empty expanse that had surrounded the post building was covered with a huddle of tents. There was a crowd of chattering Indians and Eskimos at the water's edge, and amongst them Utik stood, grinning hugely.

KABLUK OF THE ESKIMO

I went ashore amid a medley of shouts from my friends. Drollet, the factor, shook my hand fervently, and I introduced my assistant, Berthe. We went up to the post together, with a crowd of no-good "White Men" at our heels. The season had been unusually good, and Drollet was glad to be going out at the end of a peak year. It was a feather in his cap.

Drollet and Thevenet were both going out. They were glad, and we all made merry until the *Stord* pointed her prow toward the north, heading seaward.

To the fur trader in the North the visit of the steamboat is the beginning of the new year. I was determined to make it a successful one, and with Berthe I settled down to work.

There was the bartering with the Eskimo and Indian hunters, the inspection of the bundles of pelts, the sorting of them, the inventories to be taken, and the task of keeping peace among the primitive inhabitants who, I knew from experience, hated each other.

More than ever I learned to admire the Eskimo. He was clean in comparison with the Indian, and wise: a philosopher of the Arctic wilderness.

I was in the store-room one morning when a young Eskimo came in, bearing a bundle of fox pelts on his shoulder. He dropped them to the floor.

"Kabluk," he said, smiling widely. "*Chimo.*"

I looked up from the account-book which I was totalling up, and found myself gazing into the eyes

AI'VUK THE WALRUS

of Uyarak, nephew of Akpek. He reached his hand out, white-man fashion, and shook mine.

"*Chimo,* Uyarak," I answered, and glancing at the pelts I added, "*Kimoik,* the fox, has been plentiful this year."

"Aha, many have fallen in my traps."

"That is good."

In Ungava the *kimoik* or white fox fur is the most abundant, and it was the medium of exchange used at "The Fort"—the money of the country. Akpek's nephew lifted his bundle of furs to the counter.

"This man is very hungry for tobacco," he said. "He likes the taste of smoke very much."

"*Takka, takka,*" I grunted, holding a silver fox pelt up into the sunlight so that I could inspect its vivid sheen. It was a beauty.

"Many twists of tobacco for this," I went on, laying the fur carefully aside.

"How many?"

"So," I held up my ten fingers.

"Good," grunted Uyarak, taking a light for his pipe. I rapidly skimmed through his catch.

"What do you want?" I asked, jerking my head toward the shelves with their loads of merchandise.

"Tobacco," he returned succinctly.

"All tobacco?"

"Aha! That is what my people want."

A small party of Naskopies entered, bringing

bundles of marten and beaver furs. They gossiped loudly, laughing in a silly fashion. I kept my eye on them, for they were as crooked as the hind leg of a caribou.

"Wait," I said to Uyarak. "I want to talk with you."

With a disdainful look at the Naskopies, the Eskimo turned to a window that looked out toward the river. He stood there without paying further attention to the Indians, but his hereditary enemies threw evil glances at his immobile figure.

"Master, master, master," sang out the leader of the party, as I approached. "We have brought you furs; many, many furs; and we want plenty of goods for them."

"I will see," I answered curtly. "Let me look at them."

The leader, a well-built handsome buck, motioned to his men to put their burdens on the counter. With a quick movement he jerked his hunting-knife from its sheath and slit the cord that held the marten pelts together, and the raw skins flared up and slid out across the counter. Several dropped to the floor at my feet, but I made no effort to pick them up. Instead, I walked over to the place where the box of tobacco stood, and carefully placed it on a shelf where it was out of reach of thieving fingers.

"Master, master, master," cried the Indian. "I think I will have a plug of tobacco."

AI'VUK THE WALRUS

"All right, all right," I answered. "I will give it to you after I look at the furs."

The Indians were crafty beggars, but I soon got on to them. I found them to be inveterate grafters and thieves, and it was from them that the no-account "White Men" at the post had learned many of their evil tricks.

After deducting the amount that they owed from the previous trading season, I supplied the remainder in stock. They spent most of the surplus on gaudy dresses for their squaws and in fancy duds for themselves. The leader of the band took a swallow-tailed coat for his share; he put it on and stalked from the building, carrying a fifty-pound bag of flour on his shoulder.

I went back to Uyarak, who had resumed his place at the Eskimo wicket. Taking a box of matches, I went rapidly through the pile of furs again, placing a match for each white fox until there was twenty in the pile. Then I started another. Where the fur was especially valuable, I gave credit for whatever number of white fox-furs I deemed it to be worth.

"That is not necessary, Kabluk," said Uyarak, as I started on a third pile of twenty. "A man is foolish not to trust his brother."

"That is so, Uyarak," I conceded. "You will take all in tobacco?"

"Aha."

The Eskimo smoked quietly while I gathered his

payment for the furs. I stacked the tobacco upon the counter in a huge heap that grew until I could hardly see over it.

"Here is plenty of pleasure for the long winter nights," I said, coming from behind the counter. "I will help you carry them to your *komutik*."

"There will be time for that, Kabluk," answered Uyarak. "I have words for you from Akpek."

"Good," said I. "I have words for you to take to him."

We transacted our business before we talked of social matters. Although Uyarak was full of delight at meeting me, and although I thought most of his uncle, Akpek the chief, we completed our trading before we gossiped.

"Akpek is returning from a journey many, many sleeps to the north, and soon will be where the trail passes through the willows. That is the word brought by Kopeak to the village."

"Aha?"

"Akpek must see Kabluk, but he had not time to come to Kabluk. He must hurry back to the village. The trail through the willows is not far. Kabluk can meet Akpek there."

"Kabluk will go," I answered. "How soon will Akpek be among the willows?"

"Two sleeps. When the sun is high in the sky."

"Kabluk will be among the willows."

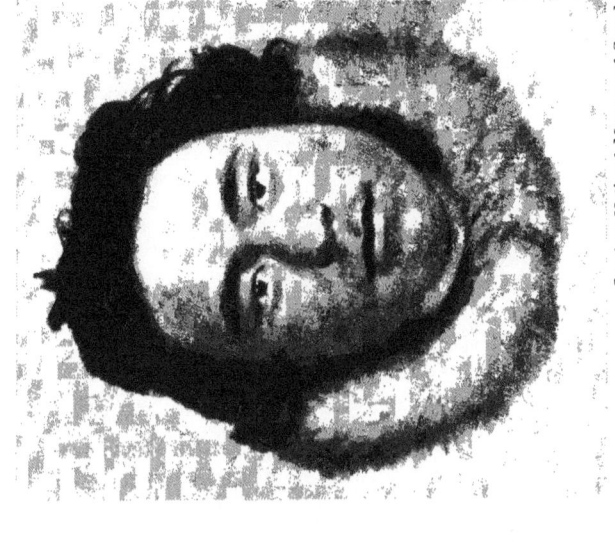

Courtesy G. Herodier

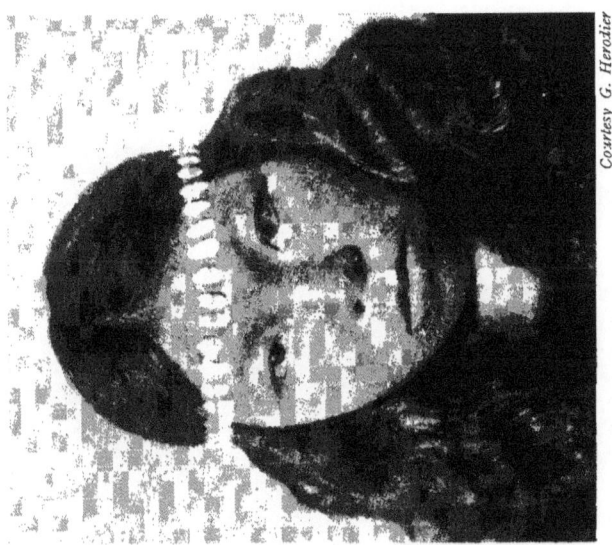

Courtesy National Museum of Canada

BRIDE AND BRIDEGROOM IN THE HAPPY VILLAGE BENEATH THE NORTHERN LIGHTS

AI'VUK THE WALRUS

The sun had not peeped above the horizon on the second day when I arose. The eastern sky was growing light with the rosy flush of coming dawn. Utik had his team ready, and with a crack of the lash we were off, heading to the north-west.

The going was hard, as the sun had softened the snow-crust, and we did not reach the appointed spot until early afternoon. Even so, we were early. Akpek and his party had not yet arrived.

Utik put up the tent, and I scouted along the trail for signs of the party's passing. When I returned, my companion had lighted a fire and was broiling venison steaks over the red-hot coals. It was late when a faint halloo came to our ears. Utik cupped his hand and answered the cry.

In a short time the first of the sledges in the party appeared around the bend in the trail. Running along beside it was Akpek, the chief. In quick succession three other *komutiks* swept into view.

"*Chimo!*" I shouted.

"*Chimo!*" answered the chief. He turned his attention to the dogs, unharnessing them and tying them apart in the willows. Night was about to fall, and he set up his tent. Then he turned to me.

"Actions before words," he said gravely.

"Aha," I said, puffing lazily on my pipe.

"The trail is bad," he went on. "The snow is soft, and much work has made the dogs tired."

"Aha, I know, Akpek."

"It is good to see you, Kabluk, but there is still work to be done. Afterwards we will talk."

The others in the party were feeding the dogs, and in a short time the savoury odour of roasting meat permeated the camp. The men ate hungrily, wolfing down their food. While we were eating, the moon, a thin crescent, appeared, and threw a silver spell over the scene; with it came a slow drop in the temperature.

In the tent of Akpek we gathered. The chief looked at me gravely. "You have travelled far?" he said.

"Aha," I answered, and I briefly outlined the events of my journey to Loon Island, my stay there, and my return to "The Fort", finishing with the customary, "I have spoken."

"Akpek and his people rejoice in your return," grunted the chief finally.

"Aha," chorused the others of the party, grinning widely.

"In the country to the west," asked Anotinoak, the tusked one, "was the hunting good?"

"On the mainland there were bear and caribou," I answered, "and along the streams beaver were found. But I saw few traces of *kimoik*, the fox."

"In twenty sleeps," Akpek announced, taking his pipe from his mouth, "my people will return to their island home. It will be the season for hunting *ai'vuk*."

AI'VUK THE WALRUS

"That is so," I admitted.

"Will you come?"

And so, once more, the subject of the walrus hunt was brought forward. It was like a persistently followed goal, distant and elusive. It was also a temptation. I meditated silently.

There was much work yet to be done at the post; but a few weeks of intensive labour would whip things pretty well into shape, and Berthe, my right-hand man, could handle things well enough until the trading season started.

"I will go," I said.

To our ears came the unearthly, weird wail of a lonely wolf, a distant, dismal sound that made me grimace. The quaveringly shrill howl died slowly away.

"*Ai'vuk* is a great warrior," grunted Anotinoak, the tusked one.

"Aha, yes," said the chief, "that is so. I remember . . ."

And he went on to tell the tale of an adventure that had first won him renown as a great hunter among his people. At that time he was a young man.

Ai'vuk, the walrus, was scarce that season, forty years past. All through the spring and early summer the hunters and scouts had not been able to find a trace of the sea mammal. The women complained loudly at the lack of leather for footgear and for the dog harness.

One hot day young Akpek took his kayak and paddled

far to the north, to a point where a sluggish but powerful current swept toward the distant shore. It was farther from the village than he had ever travelled before, but his heart was filled with courage and determination.

He pulled into shore at the tip of a promontory that divided the current into two branches. He found a streamlet of water that coursed down a bleak, rocky hillside, and ate a mess of seal blubber he had brought with him.

The water was filled with huge towering masses of ice that floated majestically into the south. Many of them were surrounded by miniature ice-fields that flared out over the water on all sides of the towering bergs.

The rugged coast swept to the south, and then cut sharply to the west, deflecting the current and its icy masses toward the yawning mouth of Hudson Bay. The eastern side of the promontory was hidden from view by immense cliffs that rose in towering masses toward the sky.

His hunger appeased, Akpek paddled to a berg that was floating by. He found that the ice fringing it was solid, and he went ashore. Pulling his kayak high up on the thick ice, he took his harpoon and surveyed his surroundings.

The ice was cut into rough, narrow troughs like furrows, and, except for the monster berg of which it formed a part, was open to view. The sun was in

AI'VUK THE WALRUS

the west, and the shadow of the berg fell athwart the spot where he stood.

It was an unlikely spot for *ai'vuk* to be found, he reflected; but, nevertheless, he circled around the base of the ice peak that cut off his view. The wind blew towards him, its gusts sending particles of snow and ice into his eyes.

Walking openly, he came to a place where the ice had sheered away, and gazed into the open water just beyond. It barred his passage and he turned to retrace his steps.

"Wa-oo!"

Forty paces away, perched upon a wall of ice, a monster walrus thrust his head high into the air. To Akpek it was like a terrible apparition. The cannon-ball head, evil eyes, and wicked tusks threatened disaster to anyone who might dare attack him.

For a moment Akpek was tempted to flee, but fear held him where he stood. The walrus, with a powerful push of its flippers, threw itself down the slope toward the open water. It was headed straight for Akpek. The Eskimo jumped back to find a firmer footing, grasping his harpoon firmly.

The monster sped down the declivity at a terribly swift pace, and Akpek saw that it would hardly be able to control its mad onslaught. If he remained where he was, he would be overwhelmed; if he moved, his prey would escape.

But one course remained. Quick as a flash, he threw himself into an ice-trough and, lying on his back with his harpoon held in readiness, he waited for the monster to pass over his prostrate form. The ice trembled under the impact of the walrus' pounding flippers and the smashing flaps of its tail.

Closer and closer came the gigantic mammal; eyes glaring with rage, whiskers bristling, and tusks gleaming in the sunlight. As it swept over the trough, Akpek thrust his harpoon upward with all of the power of his shoulders.

It was jerked from his grasp and a weltering spurt of vivid blood dashed over him. The doomed monster gave a tremendous roar, reared up, up, up, until it stood on its tail, and then toppled to the ice with a resounding thud. The harpoon had entered just above the breast bone and had slit the belly of *ai'vuk* wide open.

The disembowelled monster clawed at the ice with ponderous, ineffective strokes that rapidly subsided. Akpek found that the passage of the huge animal had almost crushed in the sides of the trough in which he lay, but he had come through unscathed.

"Aha, my children," the chief concluded. "*Ai'vuk* is a great warrior. I have spoken."

The old chief told his story as an aged hero boastfully recounts the deeds of his youth.

With the coming of dawn I turned back to the

AI'VUK THE WALRUS

post, and the chief and his party travelled on to the village.

During the succeeding days I coached Berthe in the ordinary routine of the post. Except for the no-account "White Men" we were alone, and except for an occasional band of Eskimos or Indians, who might pause briefly, we would be alone until around Easter, when there would be a brief period of trading activity. The weather was clear but icy, and I saw to it that there was plenty of driftwood put away, for I was not sure whether Berthe alone could get the hangers-on to work.

At last I was satisfied with my arrangements, and I told Utik to get the dog-team ready for an early departure on the following morning. The dawn of the winter day was still hours away when we arose.

"Adieu," called Berthe sleepily, as Utik cracked his whip.

"Adieu," I answered—and we were off.

CHAPTER IX

THE ATTACK OF THE KAYAKS

EARLY in the morning Kublo, the chief's son, brought word to the sleeping village that he had sighted a herd of walrus asleep on a drifting ice-floe.

The women, as usual, had been complaining to their men that they were in dire need of thick hides for footwear for themselves and harness for the sledges. None but *ai'vuk*, the walrus, had a hide tough enough to meet this demand; and now the time had arrived for the hunt. The women called cheerily to each other as they bustled about, preparing food for their men.

Akpek picked three of his best hunters for the expedition; I was to ride with him on his kayak. Rapidly, and without talk, the hunters got their equipment ready, discarding the ordinary harpoon for a larger one used for narwhal hunting.

As a final precaution, the hunters took care to see that their knee-boots were unlaced; otherwise the boots, being filled with inescapable air, would act as floats, forcing the wearer's head beneath the water; and, being lashed to their kayaks, the men had to be free to right themselves in case the light craft were upset. Kublo,

STEPPING INTO THEIR KAYAKS THE WALRUS HUNTERS GLIDED SWIFTLY AWAY

Courtesy Larry Wilson of Edmonton

ATTACK OF THE KAYAKS

the daring, merely smiled at such caution and laced his on tightly.

Akpek motioned me to my place. Stepping into their kayaks, the hunters glided swiftly away toward the open sea. Like shadows we moved, fleetly and silently, leaving in our wake long, regular furrows in the green waters.

Our eyes searched eagerly for the floe that carried our prey. It had drifted far to the south, and we approached it cautiously, the double paddles cutting the water without a sound. Kopeak's swaying body froze into a tense, rigid statue. He had sighted the walrus herd still asleep on the edge of the ice.

Kublo and Ernig paddled with the current to the farther end of the floe, intending to attack the tusked monsters on foot. The chief and Kopeak kept their kayaks headed directly for the ice where the walrus lay, hoping to cut off their retreat to the sea. As I lay outstretched behind Akpek, on the smooth upper covering of the kayak, I could see nearly everything that occurred.

We were near the ice. A large head thrust itself aloft with unbelievable suddenness, and a low whistle from Kopeak, who was in the lead, announced that the beasts had scented danger. Without movement we waited. The huge head warily looked around on all sides, sniffing uneasily, and then disappeared.

Akpek and his companions held their kayaks in

position by a gentle forward and backward motion of their paddles, waiting patiently for Kublo and Ernig to make a safe landing on the south end of the floe.

The wind veered suddenly and again the great head of *ai'vuk* shot skyward. We were now close in, and I could see the creature's huge body supported on its powerful flippers; its long sinuous neck undulating uneasily; its tusked head surveying its surroundings. From across the water came the peculiar walrus grunt.

Kublo and his companion were ashore. Leaving their kayaks anchored at the edge of the ice pack, they began creeping over the floe toward their quarry. From time to time we caught a momentary glimpse of them as they topped a hummock.

By sly movements, Akpek and his partner purposely attracted the attention of the sentry; it continued to sniff in trepidation and gazed inquisitively in our direction. By now Kublo and Ernig were near their prey.

"Wa-oo! Wa-oo!" a deafening roar broke the stillness.

Alarmed and enraged, the walrus reared upright. I could see his wicked eyes, his bristling whiskers, his terrible tusks. He wheeled and charged at Kublo, who stood not twenty paces away.

Kublo feinted to the left, jumped back a pace, and, springing rapidly to the right, struck with all his strength at the half-turned back of his adversary.

ATTACK OF THE KAYAKS

Mortally wounded, the huge beast bellowed in pain as the lance-head bit at its vitals.

Akpek and Kopeak were paddling toward the floe, yelling like fiends. As I lay aft on Akpek's kayak, I yelled too. The males of the walrus herd scattered madly in all directions and the females and their young made for the sea as fast as their awkward gait permitted. Before we got to the place the herd had plunged into the sea and vanished from sight.

Although clumsy on ground or ice, there is no animal more swift and formidable than a walrus in his element. But Akpek knew that, deprived of their leader, the band would flee rather than fight. He and Kopeak paddled in the direction the herd had taken.

The walrus always rises for air in the direct line of his dive, and the hunters, swaying with an ever-increasing rhythm, sent the kayaks speeding toward the north. The moments passed and I was beginning to think the hunt was over.

Suddenly a head popped into view and others followed in rapid succession. Akpek lifted his paddle high over his head. With wild shouts and waving arms, the hunters terrified the beasts, and they submerged without getting a chance to fill their lungs with air.

Again we darted forward, following the direction of the diving *ai'vuk*. The walrus again rose to the surface; but at our first shouts, panic-stricken, they plunged into the depths again with empty lungs.

Immediately the walrus broke water for the third time. Akpek pulled off to one side, content to give me, as I lay prone behind him, a close view of Kopeak's skill with a harpoon.

The hunter paddled toward a massive male and stopped within a few feet of it, watching alertly. The fatigued animal, aware of impending danger, dived slowly; baring its enormous back.

With lightning force, Kopeak hurled his harpoon into the bent body of the walrus. The lance struck home. A great spout of bright red blood spurted into the air and a bellow that seemed to shake the very depths broke the silence.

The walrus plunged, jerking the harpoon line, with its inflated bladder, clear out of sight. With backward strokes of his paddle, Kopeak retreated hurriedly from the danger zone.

Now under water, now at the surface, the beast struggled. Over and over it rolled, dark back and lighter belly; pounding the surface of the sea with terrible blows of its powerful tail. In a sudden access of insensate fury, the dying monster churned the water into a froth of flying spume and dived for the last time.

A heavy swell spread outward from the spot where the walrus had taken its final plunge. It caught Kopeak unawares and capsized his kayak; but with a strong and timely stroke with the flat blade of his paddle, he righted himself.

ATTACK OF THE KAYAKS

We were alone on the vast expanse of the sea. The float bobbed to the surface and like a magnet it drew us to it. In the depths the carcass of our quarry loomed, swaying idly in the swell from the billows above. We lashed the kayaks together for added buoyancy and, uniting our strength, we slowly heaved the huge body to the surface. The kill, fastened to the sterns of the kayaks, trailed along behind us, its huge, inert bulk swaying gently in the waves.

It was getting late. The land breeze, a bad omen in the summer, was beginning to blow. It was time to be starting homeward with our valuable burden.

"Surely Kublo has made a kill," said Akpek, puffing at his stone pipe.

"Aha, yes," I answered. "I saw him plunge his harpoon."

"*Emarha*—maybe," quoth Kopeak laconically. "The village will tell."

With a faster beat of the paddles, we wallowed along, dragging our prize in our wake. Kopeak was proud of his kill, the first of the season, and from time to time he threw a glance over his shoulder.

I had drowsed off when a distant shout aroused me. We had already rounded the promontory and the tents of the village stood out in sharp relief against the sky-line.

The villagers were all lined along the shore, grinning; the dogs, scenting a kill, howled loudly. As we neared the shore the men came climbing down the bank to greet us, and their skilled eyes appraised the kill and read the story of the day's events in our faces.

Not a question was put to us. Instead, they helped pull the kayaks ashore and dragged the carcass of our quarry to the edge of the ice, it being taboo to cut up a walrus on land.

Our prize was a monster over twenty-five feet in length, and it weighed more than two tons. The women set to work lifting the precious hide with their rounded knives, and the men busied themselves cutting up the carcass. Hedging them in, the dogs squatted in a circle, waiting patiently for scraps.

With Akpek I went to his dwelling for a bite to eat. At the threshold of the tent, Nayume stood with Amaluke. They grinned in welcome, and we smiled back.

"Aye, hullo," said the chief, gently pinching the little girl's cheek.

"Ha," mumbled the child bashfully.

We entered the tent. Nayume, realizing that we were hungry and thirsty and tired, centred her attention upon our immediate needs, and turning to her husband, she asked:

"Is it permitted to take off Akpek's boots? I will dry them by the fire outside."

Puffing placidly on his ancient stone pipe, the chief allowed her to attend and remove the boots. Finding that his socks were damp, she removed them also

ATTACK OF THE KAYAKS

and put on fresh ones, which she brought out of a round skin sack that stood in a corner. Her wifely duties done, she turned her attention to me. With a shake of my head, I told her not to bother, that I was going down to the shore again.

"I am sorry, my husband," said Nayume, bringing in a stone pot full of hot soup. "There is nothing left of the seal meat I cooked this morning."

"It does not matter," rejoined Akpek. "To-night we will feast on *ai'vuk*."

Outside, the August sun was declining fast. Punaluk, "the fading month", when the leaves and moss take on rusty colours, was at an end; and soon the ice would begin to form on the ponds. But it was still very hot and the flies were wickeder than ever.

While we were still eating our soup, several of the men came in, bearing the chief's portion of the kill; the head, forequarters, entrails, and the left foreflipper, together with a portion of the ribs.

Satisfied with his meal, Akpek leaned back against the soft sacks behind him, wiping his mouth and short beard with a grasping motion of his right hand.

"And where is Kublo, our son?" asked Nayume, when she had finished her household tasks.

"Far to the south," grunted Akpek.

"Then he will not be here for the feast."

"We will feast again—when he returns."

"Aha," I interjected. "He is a mighty hunter."

"That is good," commented Nayume; she went outside to begin the preparation of the food for the coming feast. In the tents of the hunters, where the vast chunks of walrus had been taken, the women were busying themselves preparing large quantities of food.

Nayume was the best cook in the village, and to her was entrusted the special task of looking after the delicacies. She was being helped in her work by some of the other women, and I paused to look. One was chopping brain and blubber together; another was cutting the liver into slices, dipping the pieces in a pot of boiling salt water, and placing them with blubber in a covering of sewn walrus hide.

The tastiest dish was prepared by Nayume's own hands. She cut a slab of fresh walrus hide into very small pieces, and cooked them in a pot of salt water with the heart and entrails of *ai'vuk*. It was a dish that appealed to the Eskimo palate.

At Kopeak's tent the soup was being compounded. The broth that remained in a pot in which walrus meat had been cooked was brought to a boil, and into it Kopeak's wife was pouring cold blood. She stirred the mixture constantly.

Care was taken that no seal meat had been mixed with the walrus flesh, for that is taboo. More important still, no land food might be mixed with the meat of the sea animals, for that would bring bad luck to the whole village.

Courtesy National Museum of Canada

AFTER THE BATTLE WITH AI' VUK THE WALRUS, THE CHILDREN OF THE NORTH ARRAY THEMSELVES FOR THE TRIUMPHAL DANCE

ATTACK OF THE KAYAKS

There was meat to eat, cooked or raw; delicacies to give a relish to the meal; and plenty of steaming soup to drink. In Akpek's tent there was much merriment. The chief sat on a mat of sealskin and feasted on the contents of the walrus' stomach, a mess consisting principally of half-digested mussels. These Akpek ate raw.

In each of the tents where the food had been prepared a little girl acting as messenger was dispatched from tent to tent, carrying a bowl of hot soup here, a morsel of heart there, and a titbit of rump somewhere else.

"A-ya-aya-ya."

From the darkness rose the chant of boys and girls impatient for the dance to begin. The chorus was monotonous; and, at times, the voices dropped an octave or shifted into another key without ceasing. Over all sounded the beats of the double drum.

The elders were now arriving, and they added their voices to the merry clamour, singing at the top of their lungs. I went to the dancing-place with Akpek; and as we came up there was a swaying of young bodies, with odd gesticulations of the arms and a stamping of feet in a rhythmic measure.

A circle of large stones surrounded the spot, and a moon at the full flooded it with an ethereal loveliness. Akpek took a seat, with Tickek, the shaman, on his right. I sat on his left. With our arrival the "Sculping Dance" started.

KABLUK OF THE ESKIMO

The youngest son of Kopeak, simulating the dead walrus, was lying in the centre of the circle with outstretched arms and legs, with his body covered with a skin.

Into the open stepped Kopeak and he began to mimic the hunt with extravagant movements and grimaces. His eyes rolled fantastically as he peered searchingly around for the animal he sought, brandishing an imaginary harpoon in his clenched right hand.

"To-day for *ai'vuk* I am hunting in my kayak," he sang. It was an incantation and he chanted it now high, now low, trying to render his voice strange and formidable.

Grotesquely, he danced around and around the fierce denizen of the sea, rushing furiously upon it and dealing repeated blows with his imaginary harpoon. Pretending to be tired from his terrible struggle, he changed the burden of his plaint.

"Tired I am, very," he chanted in a rhythmical singsong. "Hard have I killed."

The audience followed his every motion intently, and accompanied the performance with appropriate vocal interpretations. The beat of the drum and the voices rose in volume and the chant rolled out across the vast solitude of the night, echoing back from distant ice masses floating on the silent ocean. Kopeak, as the volume of sound reached a crescendo, rose to his fullest height and, throwing back his head, glared fiercely around him.

ATTACK OF THE KAYAKS

Instantly the tempo changed and the dance took on another character. The dancer was a man who sang of his love for a girl; he had travelled many a moon to get valuable furs to win her favour; farther than any other men he had gone, trapping the fox, killing the caribou, and fighting with the terrible beast he has slain.

"A-ya-aya-ya."

Over and over the audience chanted the refrain in low tones to the caressing murmur of the drum, assuring the dancer that his adventures are being recognized. His hardships did not matter; he had rare furs and hides, many of them; he is rich and will elope with the girl of his choice.

The dancer stopped his recital. The throbbing of the drum ceased, and the chants of the audience died away. Caught in the spell of the scene, I sat motionless, as did those around me. In the silence I could hear the distant swishing of the waves on the beach. A thrall seemed to hold all in its grip.

The dancer was the first to move. Slowly he reached for his hunting-knife. The time for skinning the hide had arrived. Kopeak tested the knife on his finger and murmured an incantation over it. The spectators watched him closely and critically as he slashed at the skin, rolling it with each cut of the knife. With a final slash, he rose to his feet and, holding his trophy aloft, congratulated himself on the glory and good fortune that was his.

Coming to life, the supposedly dead animal jumped wildly to his feet and made off, leaving the now valueless skin in the dancer's hand. Kopeak comically scratched his head and with a gesture of dismay threw the skin to one side; the dance was over.

The audience howled with laughter at the turn the dance had taken, and while the men loitered to discuss matters, the women hurriedly returned to their tents to warm up food for another round of the feasting, and the rest of the night was passed in talking, joking, and gambling.

CHAPTER X

KUBLO GOES TO AURORA BOREALIS

It was the day after the festival.

Gorged with walrus meat, the villagers still slumbered in their tents. Only the old chief himself, growing anxious for the return of his son, paced to and fro along the beach, his movements followed by the equally anxious Nayume. I walked beside Akpek in silence.

As the day lengthened, the chief's uneasiness communicated itself to others, until, as the sun reached its highest point, there were dozens of eyes watching the distant sky-line from where Kublo and his friend Ernig should come.

A mere speck against the background of sea and sky announced the return of the hunters. As the kayaks slowly came nearer, it was seen that one, trailing along in the rear, seemed to be unoccupied, and the lone paddler was approaching with difficulty. The keen-eyed Kopeak was the first to guess at the truth.

"One man paddles," he cried. "One lies flat on the other kayak. It is illness, or perhaps a wound."

Old Nayume grasped the hunter's arm.

"Who paddles?" she demanded, her eyes bespeaking the fear that dragged at her heart.

Shading his eyes with his hand, Kopeak looked again—a long, earnest gaze. Slowly his eyes turned to meet those of the fearful mother.

"It is Etnig who paddles," he announced.

The old woman crumpled, but her voice spoke up bravely.

"Kublo—does he still live?"

"His face is hidden," returned Kopeak. "A skin robe wraps him. He is lashed to his kayak."

No further explanation was needed. All present knew that the son of the old chief was coming home for the last time. The bereaved mother raised her voice in lamentation, but the chief drew himself up to his full height and stood alone. Wordless, he watched the slow approach of the kayaks.

The entire village now thronged the beach. The men were gloomy and apprehensive; the women quiet and fearful. The younger children clung to the garments of their mothers, awed by the unwonted tension that held the women silent. A dog, scenting death, lifted its head on high and howled mournfully; one by one the others followed, and in united crescendo howled their sad chorus.

Slowly the men, led by the shaman, clambered down the bank. On their faces were looks of fatalistic resignation, and with bent heads they brought the kayaks ashore.

Tickek, the conjurer, stepped forward. A thong of sealskin was fastened around his wrist to ward off sickness, fur charms hung on his clothing, and the feet of birds adorned his neck.

As majestically as his own fears allowed him, the shaman, armed with his magic amulets, examined the body; he listened for heartbeats through a long tube; and, pronouncing an incantation, tapped the head of the dead man with a bone to see whether his spirit did not wish to re-enter the body. Then he ordered the men to convey the body to the chief's tent.

As the sorrowful procession wended its way into the village, I motioned to Ernig to remain. Akpek watched until the body was in the tent; he listened for a moment to the terrible wailing that had already started; he turned away and stared out over the water.

"*Ayunamat*," he said resignedly—"it cannot be helped."

"Aha, yes," answered Ernig. "He is now in the world of light and happiness; aurora borealis has enfolded him. May his hunting be good."

"How came this sad event?" I queried.

"Hard did Kublo strike with his keen harpoon," began Ernig, and he went on to tell of the accident.

The walrus Kublo had harpooned was the leader of the herd, a mighty monarch of the northern seas, and in spite of his mortal wound, he went for his assailant. With outstretched neck *ai'vuk* came on, thrusting himself forward with violent beats of his flippers, and the whole ice-field resounded with the terrible lashing of the maddened animal's enormous tail.

Ernig saw nothing further of what had happened to Kublo. He had pursued his own quarry over a hummock of ice, dealing it a blow in a vital spot. Its death throes subsided, and with each slackening of the line he drew the creature farther from the edge of the ice. Bringing *ai'vuk* within easy reach, he finished him off with well-directed thrusts of his deadly lance.

Pleased with the results of his efforts, he called to Kublo. Receiving no answer, he set out to look for his comrade. Retracing his steps, he made his way cautiously toward the north, concealing his approach at every turn lest his sudden appearance should drive Kublo's victim to greater fury.

The silence, however, filled his breast with foreboding. An area of trampled, bloodstained snow stopped him in his tracks. His skilful eye read him the story.

Kublo had evaded the monster's rush easily. Foiled in his attempt to reach his enemy, the dying walrus had turned and made for the sea. The strong harpoon line bent like the string of a bow. Mustering all of his strength, Kublo had braced himself firmly against a block of ice and tried to hold the struggling creature.

THE WOMEN WERE QUIET AND FEARFUL
"KUBLO—DOES HE LIVE?"
"HIS FACE IS HIDDEN," REPLIED KOPEAK

KUBLO GOES

The whipping line had jerked from his hand and the anchor shaft had torn loose. In a desperate effort to save his precious harpoon and lines, Kublo had thrown himself on the shaft. Like an angry snake the writhing cord had whipped around his feet. The walrus plunged from the ice's edge into the sea and man and beast vanished in the reddened waters.

Ernig followed the trail of blood to the water's edge, noting the scraping marks of the dragging shaft and the fragments of Kublo's garments that marked it.

He reviewed the situation without emotion. Seeking a point of vantage, he viewed the broken ice-field and the open sea. To the east the death trail ran, toward a bay in which hanging ice caused an eddy. The body of Kublo had to be taken to the land of the Iglulik for burial, if the spirits were to be appeased, and in the whirlpool he hoped to find a trace of it.

Returning to the inlet where the kayaks were beached, Ernig pushed his into the water and paddled his way slowly along the edge of the pack. There was not a trace of hunter and hunted to be found, and after hours of fruitless search he decided that *ai'vuk* had dragged Kublo to the bottom of the sea.

It was hard for him to believe; Kublo was a smart hunter and surely would have managed to free himself from the line before he reached the water. Had he been knocked unconscious, the icy water would have revived him sufficiently to free himself. It was then that

Ernig remembered the warning of the women who had admonished Kublo for not unlashing his sealskin boots.

The walrus in its plunge had carried Kublo under the water, and his boots, being tight and full of air, had forced him to float head downwards. Thus he had drowned.

"*Ayunamat,*" Ernig ejaculated—"it cannot be helped."

Saddened at the fate of his companion, Ernig decided to return at once to the village, bearing the sad news to his people. But he did not forget the needs of his fellows. The precious hide of *ai'vuk* was needed to make comfortable boots for the winter and to replace the old dog-harness with new.

Before leaving, he again mounted to the highest point on the ice for a final survey of his surroundings. The lowering sun awed his superstitious soul and he hurriedly departed, dragging the carcass of his kill and Kublo's kayak in his wake. A cross-current carried him to the south.

The drift carried him sideways, and he was unable to keep the bow of his light craft directed toward his objective. So unequal did the struggle prove that he abandoned the idea of reaching land at the selected spot, and deliberately turned downstream. Fatigued by his fruitless exertions, he decided to land on a convenient ice-floe to eat and rest.

Landing on a small pack, he saw a dark object

KUBLO GOES

floating in the swirl of an eddy. A booted foot, agitated by the swell, beckoned to him, and peering over the ice's edge he found himself gazing on the lifeless body of the chief's son, floating head downward in the green depths.

A spasm of superstitious fear swept over Ernig at the ghastly sight. Fearless of death, he scarce dared to look upon the dead. Loth to touch the body, he lashed it to the side of his kayak beside the walrus, and hastened with the current towards the distant southern shore.

An offshore wind rose, bringing with it cold sleet and a heavy sea, and in the distance Ernig could hear the dull reports of breaking ice. A dim twilight fell and with it came a thick squall that obliterated both land and sky.

Throughout the night Ernig paddled, veering here and there to avoid floating blocks of ice that passed like grim shadows. The weird procession tossed uneasily on the dark waters, making a scene so ghostly that Ernig shuddered at the very thought of his ghastly plight.

The howling of the gale blowing in his teeth in no way lessened his terror, and he could not shake off the feeling that some approaching disaster threatened him. However, he took courage as he remembered the words oft spoken by his father.

"He who encounters head winds will live a long time,"

he muttered over and over, in cadence with the swing of his paddle.

Ernig's strength waned with the night, and his mind became peopled with shadows and phantoms, which he vainly tried to dismiss with incantations to Torngak, his familiar friendly spirit. The urge to abandon the corpse was strong, but, recalling that the spirit of the dead lingered on earth for three days and had great powers for good and evil, he passively accepted his lot.

Through the half-light of the dawn a dark and barren coast appeared. He landed in a little cove, stiff, famished, and exhausted. His first thought was of his duty to the dead, and he searched for a suitable site where the body might rest.

High above the water-line he found a fitting spot. Turning the corpse face downwards, that it might not meet the glance of a living man, he gently raised it and carried it to the selected place. He reverently put his inert burden upon the ground, covered the head with his best caribou skin, and sat beside it for a time, brooding over the form of his departed comrade.

Having appeased Kublo's spirit, the hunter returned to the beach. Cutting a slab of flesh from the carcass of the walrus, he ate ravenously, until his thirst urged him to find fresh water.

Drawing the kayaks high up on the dry sand, he anchored the walrus to a large rock. Not until then did he think of rest. He cast himself on the sand, but his sleep was peopled by spirits and demons, and he tossed uneasily.

The sun was well above the horizon when he awoke. He prepared the kayaks for the trip back to the village, leaving the walrus fastened to the rock so that it could be picked up later. When everything was in readiness, he brought Kublo's body to the shore and lashed it to the back of the dead man's kayak.

Seizing his paddle, Ernig set out for home. He kept in close to the shore to evade the mighty current that had swept him southward, and scarcely an hour had passed when he turned into the waterway that separated the island from the mainland.

"*Taimuk*—that is all," he finished. "I have spoken."

The chief said not a word. He turned and walked toward the village, and we followed a short distance to the rear. A hole had been cut in the wall of the tent to allow the dead man's spirit to escape. The women had hastily cut up their finest deerskins to make sepulchre garments, and Nayume had already dressed her son in them for his final appearance in this world.

A tomb had been prepared on the mainland, on the top of the hill, an oblong, walled enclosure of stones, several feet high. The bottom of the sepulchre was lined with soft mosses. In the tent all was ready too; and with the coming of evening the burial would take place.

In the tent the women beat their breasts and tore their hair, wailing heart-rendingly in their terrible grief. In an endless stream, the villagers came to the tent of sorrow, lamented with the saddened family, and departed, to return later.

Accompanied by the elders of the village the shaman came to the abode of death to perform the rite of "head lifting", in order to settle how Kublo had come to his death. But the head was heavy, the body rigid; and he expressed no opinion.

Outside the men spoke in low tones of Kublo's many virtues: of his power, strength, and fearlessness; of his skill in the hunt; and now even his former enemies spoke of him only in the highest of terms.

As the sun dropped toward the horizon, the men gathered together the belongings of the deceased. Some of the things they smashed, and in others they bored holes, so that no one would be able to use them again.

Twilight descended, and the body was drawn out through a hole at the rear of the tent. The attendants stopped up their left nostril with moss or grass to avoid contamination from the corpse, and the procession started for the place of burial.

Carried by four men, the body was taken to the shore and placed on the back of Akpek's kayak for removal to the mainland. The chief took his place, and with his only son lashed to the stern of his kayak, the chief paddled slowly across the channel.

KUBLO GOES

Wrapped in heavy deerskins, the body was deposited in the grave. Beside it were put the fire-stone, the knife, and the broken utensils. Stones were piled over the corpse until it disappeared from sight, the dead man's paddle was set in an upright position, and his kayak, harpoon and other weapons were in turn placed atop the crude sepulchre.

Four hours later—not having attended the funeral—I saw the first of the mourners returning. The women followed the men, with the hoods of their parkas drawn down over their heads. At the grave, two of Kublo's best friends remained to weep and howl.

The mourners threw away the mittens and boots used during the ceremony, and Akpek's tent was removed to another site. Through the night I wandered along the shore, unable to sleep, listening to the cries and wails of the villagers; and the sad howling of the dogs mingled with the long-drawn calls of despair, borne to my ears on the wind, from the mourners at the tomb.

The period of mourning lasted for full six days. During that time there was no hunting or travelling by the men, no sewing by the women, and no sharp-edged instruments used, in order that the wandering ghost should not be injured or disturbed.

Each day Akpek and Nayume visited the grave. The villagers had placed offerings of food and clothing there. With Uyarak, a nephew of Akpek's, I visited the spot. There were many tracks of wolves in the neighbourhood, and around the tomb the circling of restless animals had trod a deep path that seemed to shut off the deceased from his past.

The time of mourning passed, and the village resumed the even tenor of its ways. The chief was as kindly as ever, but his accustomed gravity of manner had deepened. I had seen little of him during the ceremonies that attended the death of his son, but now I resumed my place as a member of his home.

"My heart is heavy, my father," I said, troubled at the air of sadness that still pervaded the household.

"Your heart should not be heavy, Kabluk, my son," Akpek answered. "*Ayunamat*—it cannot be helped."

"Kabluk our son," put in Nayume. "He shall be son to us now."

"Aha," said the patriarch. "The woman is right. Our tent is your tent; our igloo is your igloo. What is ours is yours."

"That is good, my father," I answered; "and what is mine is yours, also."

I looked steadily at the old chief's weather-hewed features, and the message of peace and kindliness that I found pictured there gave me a boundless happiness. I was the son of Akpek the chief. I was content.

CHAPTER XI

"THE SILLY FRIVOLITIES THAT MAKE YOU LONG FOR THE GAIETY OF PARIS"

"I TELL you, Bert," I said, "it was the most exciting thing I ever saw. That damned walrus looked as big as this house, and when it turned and charged—ah, it was magnificent! And terrible.

"The hunter evaded the monster's rush with a quick leap to one side, and as it went past he launched his harpoon at its broad back. Down it went; only to rise and fall again and again, trying to get at its tormentor.

"*Sacre!* It was a sight that I never will forget."

Berthe shrugged his shoulders resignedly and said, "There are fairer scenes than that."

"What, *mon ami*, do you care nothing for the grandeur and nobility of the spectacles of this wonderful northland? Is it possible that you do not thrill to the bravery and skill of its people?"

"*Oui, oui,*" answered Berthe significantly. "But what I long for is the magnificence and beauty of La Belle France, our homeland. You seem to have forgotten its glories in this savage wilderness of snow and ice."

"*Non, mon ami, non*; but I have lost, I must confess, all desire for the silly frivolities that make you long for the gaiety of Paris. The beautiful *femmes*—what are they? Nothing but perfumed, pampered dolls; of little use to themselves or others. Here only in this 'savage wilderness', as you call it, have I found the real woman. The woman who stands beside her man, through good fortune and bad; who breeds his children; who tends his hearth . . ."

The door opened, cutting short my sermon. It was one of the no-good "White Men" who entered.

"What is it?" growled Berthe.

"Naskopie with furs at store," said the Eskimo imperturbably.

"You look them over, Bert," I said. "I want to finish this letter."

Berthe nodded glumly and followed the messenger from the room.

It was months since the tragical walrus hunt, but still I thought about it always.

". . . *my sweet, it was terrible the way those poor people carried on at the death of the chief's son* (I continued my writing). *Only he, Akpek, rose above the terrible catastrophe that had swept a desolate emptiness, an emptiness that could never be wholly filled, into his life.*

That night I was on the shore when the flotilla of death began its journey across the strait, bearing the body to the

"SILLY FRIVOLITIES"

mainland for burial. In the lead paddled Akpek, with his son's corpse lashed to the afterpart of the kayak.

The dark water and lowering sky depressed my already fallen spirits, and I watched with a leaden heart. "Charon crossing the River Styx," I thought to myself, bitter at the unpredictable cruelty of nature, of life, of everything.

Upon the chief's return I went to him. Not a word did we say, but he read what was in my heart and was glad. I was glad too. I saw that the lightning had struck the oak with its withering blast, but its proud old heart withstood the battering magnificently. My heart swelled with the knowledge, and I was proud to own the chief as first among my friends.

It is indeed difficult to give you an idea of the nobility of Akpek in words, but when I say that I regard him as I would my father, were he alive, you will have some measure of my love for him. And you, too, will love him, my sweet. He lives to see you.

Ah, you two are my only loves in the whole wide world. And I think only of the day when you will come to me. In the morning the Stord will start its long journey back to—civilization? This letter will go with it, bearing my love.

I will come for you soon.

The door opened and Utik came in. He waited until I signed and sealed the letter and turned to him.

"*Agolukok*," he said, using the Eskimo word for "Boss", "outside there is a man to see you."

"What does he want?"

"To see you."

"Has he furs?"

"Aha."

"Tell him to go to the store-room. I am busy."

"He say, '*Chimo*. This man wants to talk to Kabluk.'"

"Eh?" I ejaculated, looking up from my account book. "Is he from Akpek's village?"

"Aha."

"Why didn't you say so," I said angrily.

"The *agolukok* did not ask," he answered, looking at me comically in his distress.

"All right, all right. Show him in."

It was Uyarak. "*Chimo*," he said.

I lighted my pipe and he lighted his. I waited for him to speak, puffing lazily. The room became hazy with smoke.

"This man has come from his uncle," he said finally.

"That is good."

"This man's uncle goes to hunt *nanuk*, the great white bear."

"Good."

"In many sleeps the hunt will start."

"How many?"

"Count the fingers of your hands five times."

"Aha?"

"Then will the hunting-party leave Akpek's village for the north."

"That is good."

"SILLY FRIVOLITIES"

"Then you will come," he asked, knocking the dead ashes from his pipe.

"Aha. I will be there."

There was much to be done at the post and I did not get away at the time I expected to. I sent Utik to the village with a message for the chief, telling him that I would meet him at the mouth of the Koksoak River about the middle of December.

The chief and his party were at the appointed place several days before I came, and we went to sleep with everything set for an early start in the morning. It was still dark when we arose. The river where we were was very swift, and in spite of the intense cold it had not entirely frozen over. Because of that, Akpek delayed our departure until daylight.

The dogs were harnessed and we went down to the river's side. Akpek motioned to Kopeak. Pulling the hood of his parka as high as he could to protect his face, the young Eskimo threw himself down at the edge of the ice and began rolling over and over across the river.

He kept his body rigid as it rotated, but since his shoulders were larger than his feet the upper part of his body covered more ground than the lower section, making his path describe a series of large curves instead of a straight line. He swung in several large "S" curves before he finally reached the other shore.

Getting to his feet, Kopeak shouted that the ice

was safe enough if the dogs travelled fast. Akpek took the lead; I followed him close behind, running alongside the sledge and leaning upon it as much as possible, to distribute the weight more evenly. I was careful not to lift my feet high off the ice as Akpek had warned me that a heavy jar might crack it. All went well and we reached the other side safely.

The second and third teams followed without mishap, although I could see the ice bending under their weight and water spurting up in their wake. They travelled so fast that the ice did not have time to crack, however.

There was but one more sledge to make the difficult crossing. It belonged to Anotinoak, the tusked one. He cracked his whip, yelling, "*Huit*, go!" The dogs jumped forward at a full gallop while we called encouragingly to them.

The sledge was well past the half-way mark when a trace caught in a solid chunk of ice, bringing the dogs to a slithering stop. Anotinoak cautiously walked forward to release the harness. Stepping backward toward the rear of the sledge, he again commanded the dogs to go ahead.

Again the animals jumped forward. The sudden strain was too much for the already weakened ice. It cracked with a snap and Anotinoak disappeared beneath the surface. The team, like a flash, passed from the danger zone and reached the shore.

"SILLY FRIVOLITIES"

Akpek motioned to Kopeak. He took half a dozen harpoons from the others in the party and started across the treacherous ice, laying them before him as he went, to increase the supporting surface for his weight. I watched with my heart in my mouth.

Progressing rapidly, Kopeak reached the broken ice. Reaching out his arm, he grabbed Anotinoak's hair with a tight grip. Lifting upward with all of his strength, he kept his comrade's head above water.

Anotinoak extended an arm carefully over the thin ice, testing its strength. It held, and he placed his other arm in the same way. Still the ice held firm.

Working with deliberation, he lifted a leg slowly until it rested securely on the ice on the opposite side of the hole. His other leg followed and he lay outstretched over the break in the ice. Kopeak slowly backed away.

Very slowly Anotinoak changed the position of his body and then made his way along what amounted to a bridge of harpoons.

Without speaking, the tusked one rose to his feet, shook himself, and pressed the water out of his soaked clothes. Two men set to work to build a small shelter of snow so that Anotinoak could change his wet garments.

"*Huit*!" shouted Akpek, without further ado. We started on again, knowing that they would follow us as soon as they were ready. About noon we came within sight of the great ocean. But there were no tumultuous waves dashing against the rocky cliffs. All was rigid and still; the ice extended a long way from shore. In the distance a dark line of unfrozen sea gave its limit.

From our vantage-point on the cliffs, our view embraced a vast expanse of snow-covered earth on one side, with ice-covered lakes and rivers gleaming in the dark settings of their valleys; on the other side only the uncertain shore-line of the coast met our gaze.

We headed across the ice. The salt water which remained unfrozen on the ice in spots made the road wet and slushy. The going became rough and the runners of the sledges dragged heavily. The mud caked on the runners of the *komutiks* wore away and we left deep black marks in our wake.

The weather was clear and the sun rather warm for the season. Coming around a headland, Akpek drew up sharply. A quarter of a mile away a band of seals lay basking in the warmth on the edge of the ice. Akpek picked three of his men for the hunt and sent the rest on under the leadership of Kopeak.

We took the dogs back to the shore and tied them securely so that they couldn't get loose and disturb the seals by their presence. There was scarcely any wind and what little there was fortunately came from the sea.

Without any special precaution, we walked toward

"SILLY FRIVOLITIES"

the resting amphibians until we were within five hundred paces or so, as the seal cannot distinguish clearly beyond that distance.

The seals were far from the edge of the ice, but it was impossible to tell whether or not there was an open crack near where they lay into which they would immediately plunge should they be alarmed.

A large male was acting as sentinel, and behind him the rest of the band lay sleeping. He was taking short naps, lifting his head at intervals to look cautiously around, and then he would remain quiet for a minute or so.

During the intervals we moved forward until the sentinel of the band stirred. While he inspected his surroundings for signs of danger, we crouched on our knees on the ice. We repeated our tactics until we were about two hundred feet away.

I noticed that the guardian of the band was becoming more particular in his inspections; his gaze lingered longer in our direction. But seeing that we remained motionless, he resumed his napping. Akpek, dropping to his knees, moved forward, imitating the movements of a seal, and we followed suit.

Wriggling on our bellies in the slush we zigzagged toward our quarry. I was amazed at the aptitude the hunters displayed in mimicking the movements of a seal. We approached to within fifty paces of the herd, when the going became too difficult for me;

afraid of scaring the seals, I hung back, content to watch Akpek and his men go about their jobs.

Akpek acted as guardian of his little band, and when the sentinel seal surveyed his surroundings, the chief thrust up his head likewise, gazing suspiciously at the herd of seals. During the intervals of relaxation, the hunters dragged themselves closer and closer to the band, blowing and snorting.

I waited for the moment that Akpek should signal for the hunt to begin, ready to jump to my feet and take a hand in the slaughter. There came no signal. Puffing and snuffling, Akpek and his men crept right in among the sleeping seals.

From where I stood it was impossible to tell the hunted from the hunters. The sentinel seal bobbed his sleek head to and fro in a regular rhythm, but the band slept on. I kept my eye on Akpek and was amazed to see him slither right up to the uneasy leader of the herd. He leaped to his feet and thrust his harpoon into his quarry; the seal upreared its body convulsively and dropped to the ice with a tremendous crash.

There was a rush of sleek bodies at that untoward movement, and the butchery began. Akpek moved with lightning speed, caught a seal by its flippers, dragged it away from an open crack in the ice, and brained it with the handle of his harpoon.

At the first sign of activity I had leaped to my feet and sprinted for the scene of battle, but, short

"SILLY FRIVOLITIES"

as the distance was, I got there too late. Each of the hunters had harpooned a victim, and two that tried to retreat to the sea had been stabbed to death with knives. Not a single one escaped.

Pleased with the success of the hunt, the men began to laugh at the bedraggled appearance of their comrades. Even Akpek smiled soberly as he signalled one of the men to return to the mainland for the dog-teams.

While we were busy skinning our kill, Anotinoak and his companions came up. They too had met with seal and slaughtered their share. Akpek sent them on to Kopeak with orders to halt at a convenient place and put up igloos for the party. We followed a short time later.

The camp had been made on the edge of a frozen pool, and we soon made ourselves comfortable. The whole party gathered in the largest of the igloos to eat. After we had finished the meal, the leaders of the groups recounted the events of the day. Anotinoak, being the eldest, spoke first.

"As we were travelling fast to catch up with the party," he began, in a semi-dramatic, humorous way, "I saw ice that looked good for seal holes. I thought that seal meat would taste good. The ice was smooth. The nose of the dog is keener than this man's. They had scented prey. The dogs started at a full gallop toward the air-holes in the ice.

"They were unmanageable. We turned around

and headed back to the shore. Uyarak stayed with the teams. My son and I fastened pieces of white bearskin under our boots. We marched back across the ice.

"We found two air-holes not far apart. My son took the left one. I took the right hole. I advanced until I could hear the seals snorting. As my victim snorted, I moved one pace forward. He came up again. I took another step. And so on for six times.

"I reached my place. I waited for my victim to appear. The air-holes were close together. I motioned to my son to be still. But the next snorts came from his hole. With each successive rise of his prey, he paced forward. I did not want to scare my seal. I remained perfectly still.

"We waited with harpoons poised. I was set for a hard thrust. I waited for my prey to appear. A bubble of water warned me. A sleek black head broke water. I struck hard. I got the seal right through the head. He was a big fellow. He sounded. He went down fast. I lost my mitts. The harpoon line burned my fingers.

"My son's hole stayed empty. The other seal was frightened. It plunged before my son could spear it. He came to help me land my kill. The water began to heave and bubble in the air-hole. I knew that my seal was mortally wounded. It was coming up for a final gulp of fresh air.

"SILLY FRIVOLITIES"

My son broke the thin crust of icy snow around the hole. It was big enough to pull my kill through. Together we pulled the wriggling beast out on the ice. it showed fight. But Anotinoak's harpoon is deadly to any animal that tests its thrust.

"I have spoken."

Outside the wind, wailing in fits and starts, was beginning to rise. Uyarak, who had gone outside to quiet the dogs and feed them, came in, bringing an icy gust with him. He seated himself upon a mat of caribou hide and lighted his pipe.

Akpek looked at Kopeak, who also, while away from the main party, had encountered seal.

"We too came upon seal ice," Kopeak related, "but it was away to the south. There came a splash of a diving seal. I thought it would be good to get that one. But it had been scared by our approach. It did not come back.

"There were a number of holes within a short distance. I put myself at the largest. I made it the centre of a circle. I had Uyarak drive his sledge over the other holes in the vicinity. The seals would be too frightened to come up at any of them to breathe. He drove around and around without result.

"I was just getting ready to give up. I heard a noise under me. I heard a loud snort. With all my strength, I thrust downward with my harpoon. It bit deeply. In no time at all we had our kill on the ice.

"We were happy at our unexpected success. We continued on our way. It was not far from here that Anotinoak and his men came up with us.

"*Taimuk*—that is all."

"It is well," said Akpek. "Now we will rest. To-morrow we travel far."

The morning broke dark and drear. It was snowing hard, and the drifts were piling up higher and higher. It was hard to see very far ahead, and the white mantle had blotted out all signs of the trail. We had food aplenty and Akpek decided that we would stay in our camp until the storm blew itself out.

Night came on and we still were stormbound.

CHAPTER XII

THE HUNT FOR NANUK, THE GREAT WHITE BEAR

WITH the dawn came fine, crisp, cold weather. The camp stirred early, and we were soon on our way with the chief leading. We were heading north-west, following the shore-line.

We were bound for Akpatok Island, an isolated place far to the north. The island is a gigantic block of granite, a vast immensity of bleak rock, ringed in by the ocean and flat as a table on top. It was a favourite spot for *nanuk*, the great white bear.

In a little cover on the south shore of the island we made our quarters. The Eskimos came to the island but once every two years, as during the year succeeding each hunt *nanuk* shunned the island.

There was much work to be done before the spring would come, and we settled down to igloo life. There were other Eskimos on the island, but we did not see much of them. They too had come to hunt the great white bear.

One day there was a tremendous uproar among the dogs, and Akpek went out to quiet them. The howling continued unabated, and in a short time he returned.

KABLUK OF THE ESKIMO

"Come," he said, and, turning, went outside again.

I followed at his heels. The frozen earth was bathed in a soft, weird light. Overhead was the trail of a heavenly visitor. It was Halley's Comet, a most glorious sight. The celestial visitor was a brilliant point of light. The tail swept an ever-widening swath across the sky.

Among the Eskimos there was much excitement. To them I explained that a star was passing near the earth and that its speed was so great that it left a trail of fire behind; and, taking a brand from the fire, I showed how the tail of fire behind the comet was formed. One after another they took the stick of smoking wood and waved it to and fro, watching childishly as the smoke streamed to the rear.

"But there is no fire in the tail left by the torch," said Anotinoak.

"True," I answered. "To leave fire behind it must travel much faster."

"You say it goes at great speed?"

"Aha."

"Then how is it that it does not go away?"

Taking a stick, I drew a small circle on the snow and around it I placed a much larger one; running a line from the smaller to the larger, I explained that the farther it was away from us, the longer it would remain within our range of vision.

"Aha," said Akpek, nodding wisely.

Courtesy National Museum of Canada

WHILE AKPEK HUNTS NANUK THE GREAT WHITE BEAR,
NAYUME, HIS WIFE, GOES FISHING

THE HUNT FOR NANUK

For a full week the sky remained clear and the comet was displayed to our eyes in all its glory. My companions had spread the word that there was a great magician amongst them, one who could tell the secrets of the upper world: the world of aurora borealis.

One day an Eskimo from one of the other camps on the island came to me, crying:

"*Agolukok*, to-day I have not seen my wife."

"Aha?"

"That body of fire," he shouted, shaking his fist at the heavens, "he roams around the island all night; he won't go away; and last night he went into my igloo; he was after my woman. Don't you believe so?"

I quieted him, telling him to seek his wife among her relatives; and that was the last I heard of him. He found his wife. My fame as a great medicine man, a shaman of great power, spread over the island.

The spring days were coming nearer, when an Eskimo I had never seen before came into camp.

He joined the circle, squatted around the campfire, and began to brag of his ability as a conjurer. From the way he was treated by the men I could tell that he was hated—and feared. At his approach, Akpek had left the group and retired to his igloo. I followed.

"Who is that man?" I asked.

"He is a bad-hearted man," said Akpek.

I smoked in silence. The fellow must be pretty

bad for the chief to characterize him with the strongest epithet that one Eskimo can use to another.

"Why does he come here?"

"I do not know," answered Akpek uneasily. "We do not like to see him at all."

"Let us go outside," I said, knocking the ashes from my pipe and rising.

The men made room for us around the fire, but our visitor did not budge. The fellow began to show off, trying to impress me with his power in the world of spirits. I let him rant for a while in silence.

"What can you do?" I asked at last.

"I can eat fire," said the bad-hearted one. "It is something no white man can do."

"You can eat fire, eh?"

"Aha," boasted the conjurer.

Stooping quickly, I picked a blazing chunk of driftwood from out of the fire. I thrust it at him, saying:

"Now, my man; you eat it."

He stumbled backward as the flaming brand singed his face, and turning away from us, left without another word. Akpek smiled soberly; but his men laughed heartily at the discomfiture of the faker.

The winter was gone and the day for the hunt was set. As a rule, the Eskimos are not early risers, but some of the dogs had freed themselves, and they had to be caught before we could start. The old dogs generally remain

THE HUNT FOR NANUK

around the camp and pick up any eatables they can find; the young, inexperienced ones wander away from camp as soon as they have gnawed their traces.

Kopeak, fearing that his big pup might have wandered far, was the first one up. The young dogs, not being wise in the ways of their kind, are in danger of being caught in deadfall traps. Hunger gets the better of their judgment and they go in after food; and the drop invariably cripples them.

The night had been very cold, and a thick mist had floated in from the open sea, covering the camp with an evanescent whiteness that cut our visibility to a minimum. The fog distorted distances and shapes, and I elected to go with him.

Kopeak, who knew the track of every one of his animals, took up the trail of his wandering pup. We followed the tracks down to the shore; they ran along the shore-line for a while and then turned toward the open sea. The sea-ice was slushy and we soon lost sight of our trail.

It was not yet light enough to see any distance, and the fog made it difficult to discern objects even near at hand. We turned back to the camp, going in a different direction from the one we had followed on our way out.

Suddenly my companion halted and I halted too. Toward the sea the fog had lifted slightly and revealed a huge animal seated on the top of a large ice hummock. A polar bear, I thought.

KABLUK OF THE ESKIMO

"*Nanuk*," whispered Kopeak, half-questioningly.

Motioning to me to follow, Kopeak cautiously retraced himself until we had reached cover, and then he started for camp on the run. In a short time the party, armed with lances and knives, were ready to set out. Kopeak led the way, armed with a powerful bow.

We reached the shore-line before we sighted our quarry. It was still seated on the ice, a monstrous figure on its pedestal, looming against the swirling curtain of fog. Our dogs howled excitedly.

Fitting an arrow into the bowstring, Kopeak took careful aim and shot it at the breast of the huge beast. The missile sang through the air but the monster did not shift its position.

The men moved forward cautiously, lances and knives ready for immediate action. The nearer we came to the beast, the more mysterious it seemed. Its body seemed to shrink and it darkened perceptibly. I rubbed my eyes at the phenomenon.

We were almost up to the animal before sharp-eyed Kopeak recognized his missing puppy. The mirage created by the fog had enlarged the size of the dog to such an extent that at a distance of about one hundred feet it loomed up enormously, and, tinted by the intervening fog, it appeared white. Hence our mistake.

Everyone had a hearty laugh over the escapade—everyone but the pup. Kopeak made him pay for our

THE HUNT FOR NANUK

unnecessary efforts. We went back to the camp, harnessed the rest of the dogs and started out for the interior of the island.

We were hardly half an hour under way when Akpek's team crossed the huge track of a great white bear. Without pausing, he swung his sledge and followed it. The trail led down toward the shore.

At the edge of the ice the chief pulled up to discuss the situation. *Nanuk* is the largest and most powerful quadruped roaming the Arctic country; living with equal ease on land or in the water, he prefers the ice-pack most of all.

"Kabluk, my son," said the chief. "*Nanuk* is a redoubtable fighter. We will need every man to subdue him. Will you stay with the dogs?"

"My father," I answered. "I have travelled far to come to grips with *nanuk*. I am not afraid."

"Good," commented Akpek with quiet satisfaction.

We started on again, following the fresh tracks. The ice became rougher and rougher, and now high hummocks and pinnacles of snow and ice cut off our view.

At a signal from Akpek we halted again. We stopped, and the dogs were quieted. The chief pointed and, following the direction of his outstretched arm, I saw a patch of dirty white partly hidden behind a block of ice. As I watched, the object moved and disappeared from view.

KABLUK OF THE ESKIMO

Half a dozen of the adult dogs were taken from their traces; they yelped and whined eagerly, sensing the hunt; each was held in leash to keep them from running ahead and alarming the bear.

The wind was blowing from the sea; but we had to make a long detour to the windward to cut off his retreat to the open water. *Nanuk's* sight is poor, but his sense of smell is very keen; and we had no sooner arrived between him and the sea than he appeared upon a hummock, sniffing uneasily.

The long, sinuous neck was outstretched; a little head in which a pair of wicked eyes gleamed swayed continuously, searching his limited horizon for a view of his enemies; his feline, rippling body squatted motionless; his upraised forepaws stabbed at the air.

The fur of the polar bear is very valuable to the Eskimos. It has no equal as an insulator between the cold ice and the warm bodies of sleeping men; and the hide is tough and untearable; the strong hairs cannot wear out. In the North, *nanuk* is the great prize.

But the great white bear is a redoubtable antagonist. He can fight when attacked; and at times he will offer battle to man without any provocation whatever.

Sensing that escape by water was impossible, our quarry perched himself more firmly on its large, round pedestal of slippery ice and waited, snarling.

Moving in and out among the blocks of ice that impeded our vision, we almost passed by our prey,

THE HUNT FOR NANUK

when there came a warning hiss from the bear. At that frightful sound, Akpek and his men went into immediate action.

Loosing the dogs, they jumped back. The courageous animals formed a circle around the bear, snarling viciously. *Nanuk* lashed out with terrible sweeps of his taloned paws at his tormentors, but the dogs promptly retreated before his onslaughts, while those at his back dashed in, snapping at the monster's hind legs.

Nanuk dropped on all fours, his long neck poised straight before him, his flat head held low; and, thrashing with his powerful legs, he cleared a wide space around him. The dogs retreated. *Nanuk*, rising upon his hind legs again, towered up, up, up, to his full height; waving his forelegs to and fro like enormous arms, he snarled his rage and defiance.

The terrible paws clawed the air threateningly. High in the air his head towered, the huge mouth open, yellow fangs uncovered. For a moment *nanuk* stood thus, a monarch of the everlasting ice, fully ten feet tall.

The dogs ringed him in again. He fought gamely. With a single sweep of his powerful paw he disembowelled one of the dogs, flinging it twenty feet through the air. The carcass landed against the ice with a sickening thud.

Akpek made ready his bow and the others poised their lances. Advancing cautiously, the chief launched an arrow from his great bow. The arrow buried itself in the maddened brute's side. *Nanuk* scarcely seemed to notice it.

The men launched their lances with mighty throws. Two of the spears bit deeply, sticking in the flesh. *Nanuk*, maddened with the pain, tore out the weapons, leaving the head of one embedded in his hide. He looked terrible in his mighty rage, but he was helpless against the unrelenting attack that converged upon him.

There was no escape for him. Turn wherever he would, there was an enemy to harry him. He struck out with savage but impotent ardour. Again and again the lances bit into his body, sinking deeper and deeper, as the emboldened hunters crept closer; again and again the dogs sank their fangs into his faltering hind quarters.

The yellowish-white coat of the bear was stained with scarlet. Foam flecked his mighty jaws and dripped down over his chest. The snow, blood-blotched, resounded with the drumming of his mighty legs. Driven to bay, *nanuk* bellowed his rage and fought doggedly on; but he was tiring.

Stepping in close, Akpek faced the monster. The old chief poised his weapon. With a quick thrust he stabbed his lance between the beast's ribs and pierced it to the heart. The bear lunged convulsively toward him, gripping with his paws. Akpek jumped to one side, evading the murderous rush, and the fight was over.

ESKIMO ARCHERS AIMING THEIR ARROWS AT NANUK, THE GREAT WHITE BEAR

Courtesy National Museum of Canada

THE HUNT FOR NANUK

Driving off the dogs who were worrying the carcass, the men set to skinning their kill. According to custom, the precious furred hide went to the chief, he having given *nanuk* his first wound.

We got back to the camp shortly after midday. The hunt had been good, and Akpek and his men spent the rest of the day preparing the flesh and hide and in feasting.

Many more of the great white bears were to fall before Akpek and his men ere we started homeward, but no hunts were as thrilling as that first meeting of mine with *nanuk*, the king of the north.

CHAPTER XIII

THIS WOMAN HAS KILLED NANUK

THE bear hunt over, we returned to the village. There was much rejoicing, for we had brought back many of the valuable skins. The women chattered, the men smiled, the dogs howled; and there was much feasting.

I was glad to see old Nayume again. She too was glad, and expressed her gladness in many ways. She made dishes that she knew I liked, and made garments of her softest skins for my use.

At her request, I described the hunt to her. She listened with shining eyes.

"I too have killed *nanuk*," she said, as I finished.

"You!" I ejaculated in surprise.

"Aha," she said stolidly.

"With her own hands," said Akpek, smiling approvingly.

"I would like to hear about it."

"My man can tell it," answered Nayume. "I am busy."

I looked to Akpek. He spurted forth a cloud of smoke from between clenched teeth and, settling his pipe firmly in his mouth, said:

NANUK IS KILLED

"It was before she was my woman. She was married to another man, who died. She and her little baby were alone in their igloo. Besides her and the child, there was no living person around the snow-house. Her husband was away on a hunt on the ice.

"*Nanuk* had roamed the ice. He came to land. Was it hunger? Was it curiosity? None can say. It brought him to the lone igloo with stealthy steps.

"He sniffed around the place. He found the entrance. He entered.

"The baby slept. Nayume was just placing a soft blanket over the child. She heard a noise and turned around. It was *nanuk*. His wicked head was in the igloo.

"Nayume is a brave woman. She had her child to protect. A knife was at hand. She grasped it. It was all she had. Her husband had taken his heavy hunting spear with him. And the knife would not kill *nanuk* unless its blade reached the heart.

"There was no other weapon. Yet her eyes looked for one. She saw nothing but a blanket.

"Snatching the deerskin robe from the sleeping child, she threw it over the flat head of *nanuk*. She pulled it as tight as she could.

"Roaring in surprise and rage, *nanuk* tried to turn around. His body was jammed in the entrance. He was blinded. He was smothering. He was cramped. And he could not use his forepaws to tear the strange thing from his head.

KABLUK OF THE ESKIMO

"Nayume quickly dug a hole in the opposite wall of the igloo. She took up her child; she clambered out into the open. Putting the little one on the snow, she went to the great struggling animal. She jabbed with a strong sure stroke at the heart of *nanuk*. The sharp point of the long knife hit its mark.

"*Nanuk* was dead."

"Aha, my husband," said Nayume. "You tell this woman's story well."

The next afternoon I went over to the mainland with Uyarak to get some driftwood. In a clump of willows we came upon a covey of ptarmigan. Their feathers stood upright. The birds scarcely moved as we went by.

Stopping his *komutik*, Uyarak signalled to me to remain quiet. Taking his whip, he aimed carefully at one of the birds. It cracked loudly and off snapped the head of a ptarmigan. The remaining birds moved a few paces and stopped.

"Ka ka ka ka ka," they called.

Again Uyarak snapped his whip and another bird fell. It was a lively sport, and I was amazed at Uyarak's unfailing skill with his whip. Each crack of it dropped a bird. I grunted my approval.

"It is nothing," answered Uyarak. "It is not like Akpek. This man cannot handle the whip like Akpek."

"The chief—can he do better?"

"Aha."

NANUK IS KILLED

I shook my head slowly, incredulous.

"Many times have my eyes seen him," snorted Uyarak. "He is old. Even so he is better than his hunters."

In the tent of the chief I sat that night, smoking a peaceful pipe before retiring. Nayume was putting Amaluke to sleep, crooning softly to her. The domestic scene awakened a yearning in my heart and I thought longingly of a pair of tantalizing black eyes.

I was lounging in the tent the next morning when a little girl came in, bringing a skilfully made sleeping-rug which she handed to me. For a moment I thought a mistake was being made and I made no effort to accept the gift.

"Norrak's little sister brings a gift from her," explained Nayume.

Reaching out, I took the present, whereat the messenger fled without further ado. I fingered the soft caribou of which the rug was formed, at a loss as to what I was to do.

"Norrak is a strong girl," said Nayume. "She is a hard worker. She will bear many children."

"Aha," grunted the chief approvingly.

I sat silent for a time, meditating on the gift and the spirit of the giver. Rising, I went to the tent of Norrak's father.

The mother was putting the final touches to her man's footgear when I entered. I was in a quandary, not knowing just how to begin to explain what was on my mind. Norrak, the little minx, made things worse by staring at me with a peculiarly seductive smile.

"In Rome do as the Romans do," runs the adage, but my inborn principles would not allow me to trespass beyond the line of white man's decency, even though I was in a primitive village where a man can take a mate whenever and wherever he pleases.

The mother, mistaking my embarrassment, said kindly:

"We do not expect a present from you, Kabluk. When you are skilled in hunting—then you will give."

My speculations were interrupted by a hail from outside.

"Kabluk," called Norrak's brother, "here is one who needs your aid. Will you give it?"

I stepped outside, glad to end the embarrassing situation. The drilling of a stone lamp was in progress. A bow drill was being used, and I held the stone pot firmly while the artisan, head bent low, set to work. The bit scratched and squeaked with a disagreeable penetrating noise and with each turn it sank deeper.

The patience of the artisan was remarkable, and his precision and skill was nothing short of marvellous. A neat round hole appeared in the side of the bowl and, raising his head, the operator said:

"*Taimuk*—that is all."

NANUK IS KILLED

I wandered toward the shore, thinking. It was obvious that the villagers regarded myself as one of them. They were wondering why I did not take Norrak for wife.

All knew that I was womanless, and to them woman was a necessity to life and happiness. It was natural for them to anticipate my marriage to Norrak. In that way only could I get a perfect servant to cater to my wishes: someone to cook for me, to fashion and sew my clothing, to prepare the skins of my kill, to attend to the lamp, and to bear and bring up my children.

I paused near the shore to watch a group of the women netting fish in a little stream. They laughed and chattered happily, and I thought of Moose Factory, and my woman.

Noting some of the women about to shove off from the shore in an umiak, I hastened my steps. The ungainly craft had caught my interest, and I wondered how they would navigate it. The women, seeing my hasty approach, looked at me curiously.

"You are going fishing?" I queried, smiling.

"Aha," said a fat old woman who seemed to be in charge.

"I would like to go too."

The women looked at me; they looked at one another; and then they burst into hilarious laughter. "You are not a woman," grunted the old one. And without another word the party climbed aboard and shoved off.

Wondering what I had done to create all the hilarity, I returned to the tent of the chief. To him I explained the matter, asking what I had done.

Akpek smoked gravely for a few moments as he cogitated upon the matter. "My son," he said, "it is not proper for a man to travel in a woman's boat."

"Aha," I replied, nodding gravely.

I listened to the breeze sweeping through the village; the tent flap waved to and fro in regular timed movements. The chief smoked his stone pipe meditatively. Nayume, her regular household tasks done, sat at the rear of the tent, beading a section of caribou hide.

"You need a woman," she said, looking up from her work.

"Aha, my mother," I answered, thinking of the girl with snow-white skin I wanted to marry.

"Women speak foolishly many times," grunted Akpek. "Nayume is not a woman when she speaks."

The old woman gazed gratefully at the patriarch and went on with her work. Akpek rubbed his nose thoughtfully.

"Aha," he went on, after an interval of silence pregnant with things unsaid. "Nayume is right. Woman is made for man. You need a woman."

"It is time that I should speak," I answered.

"Aha?"

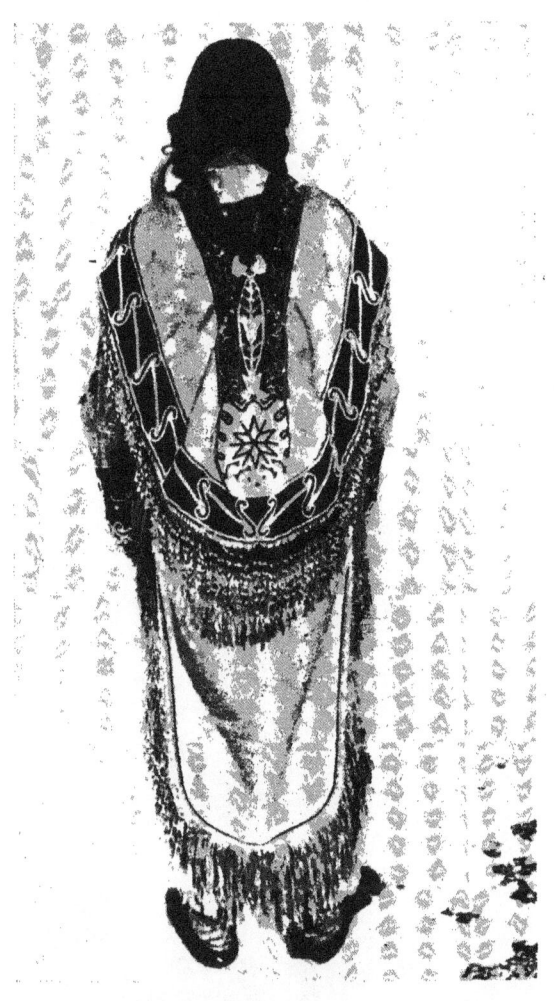

WHAT A WELL-DRESSED WOMAN WEARS AT THE BLUBBER BANQUET

NANUK IS KILLED

"Far to the west and the south, on Hudson Bay, my woman waits for me. Soon I shall go to her."

Nayume's fingers stitched faster, more nervously. In stolid, unmoving silence the chief sat on his couch of deerskins. At last he spoke.

"My son," he said, "the place you mention is many, many sleeps' travel from here. Is a woman worth the difficult journey?"

I pondered his words thoughtfully. "You have said I need a woman to make me happy, my father."

"Aha! That is true."

"Yet you do not wish me to go for her."

"My son, in the tribe there are many good strong women."

"That is so."

"They are skilled and work hard."

"That is so."

"They will bear you strong children. You may have your choice."

I did not know what to say. I did not want to hurt the feelings of my friends, and I cast about for a way out of my difficulty.

Nayume spoke:

"Norrak is a strong girl. It is evil not to take a woman who is suited to you."

I began to realize that my inaction in not taking Norrak appeared strange to the villagers. They were wondering what was the matter with me. In their eyes

I was acting indecently. Norrak too thought it exceedingly strange that I did not take her. It was time that I put the situation in its proper light.

"My father," I said, "you would have me marry one of your tribe?"

"Aha."

"Why?"

"Are you not my son; Nayume's son; our son?"

"That is true."

"Then sow your seed amongst us."

The chief stared at me solemnly; taking his pipe from his mouth, he remained immobile, awaiting my answer. I racked my head for a way out of the muddle.

"My father," I queried, "would you marry one of the Naskopies?"

"Faugh," he grunted and spat into a corner.

"Would you marry a woman of my tribe?" I asked again.

Akpek puffed slowly on his pipe and rubbed his nose thoughtfully with the back of his forefinger. For a long time he said nothing; I stared lazily into the segment of sky that was to be seen from the entrance to the tent.

"My son," said Akpek finally, "you have the wisdom of my people. I would not marry out of my people."

"And I, my father, must marry a woman of my tribe."

NANUK IS KILLED

He meditated. "She is strong?" he asked.

"Aha."

"She is a good worker?"

"In the North only the good survive," I answered.

"That is well."

And so I had the permission of Akpek the chief to take as my wife the strong-bodied, white-skinned girl who lived on the southern shore of Hudson Bay.

CHAPTER XIV

FAR SOUTH ON HUDSON BAY MY WOMAN WAITS

It was now four years since that season when first I had encountered the strong, dark Norwegian girl at Moose Factory, who was too young for marriage. As winter and summer passed, she was still too young. Each summer, when the boat came in, it brought me a letter from her, and when it went out it carried a long letter of mine to her. But a girl cannot always remain too young for marriage. The pigtailed kid of fifteen becomes the woman of eighteen. And days of July came when the *Stord* steamed across Ungava Bay and steered up the river to "The Fort", and aboard was a letter for me from the old Norwegian at Moose Factory. He told me that his daughter was now old enough for marriage and that I could come and get her. And a letter from the girl bade me journey south and fetch her away to the North as soon as I could.

"Berthe," I shouted, "I am going to get my wife!"

"*Eh bien*," he responded. "Some men are unlucky, failing to escape marriage. Some are fools, who pursue marriage, like a caribou calf that insists on making the acquaintance of a pack of wolves. But I don't blame

MY WOMAN WAITS

you. A woman will be pleasant, that is a white woman, instead of these Eskimo and Indian wenches. So go, *mon vieux*. I will take care of the trading season."

That year fox and mink were abundant. The trapping season was one of the best. That meant busy trading at the post. It also meant that I was needed at "The Fort". If I took the ship out a few days hence, and returned with my wife when the *Stord* steamed north again the following year, it would mean that I, the chief factor, would be absent from my post during the better part of a bumper trading season. What would the company think of that? No, in the North a man sticks to his post.

"I will not take the ship out," I told Berthe. "There will be work for more than one man here until the trading is over. I will stay until then."

"But this marriage?" asked Berthe.

"I will go when winter comes on. Yes, there will be no ship then. I will go overland."

"Overland, from Ungava to the southern half of Hudson Bay—and in the winter? That is a hard trip."

"Yes, I know," I replied.

The *Stord* dropped down the river, carrying a letter to the folks at Moose Factory, that in the winter I would make the overland journey for the marriage. Likewise, I informed the company officials of my plan.

During the next two months the trading was brisk, and we accumulated a mountain of pelts. In October there was a great blizzard. The winter was hard and bitter. I made preparations for a long and arduous journey, engaging a party of Indians to make the trip with me. The day for departure came and I shook hands with Berthe.

"Until summer, Berthe," I told him. "When the *Stord* returns, I will be aboard, and with me will be as strong and brave a young wife as you ever saw."

"*Au revoir*, and good luck," responded Berthe.

"Ready, Uchimau," called Ynish.

It was January and cold as an icicle. I pulled on my gloves before opening the door. My party was ready for the trail and, putting on my snowshoes, I joined the little group.

Ynish, a chief of the Naskopies, and five of his men, were to accompany me on the long overland journey to Rupert House at the lower end of James Bay. Each of the Indians hauled a flat sleigh with the exception of the chief; he had a wicked little dog harnessed to his to help him.

My Indians were all dressed up in painted deerskins with the hair inside and the skin, coloured in vivid reds and blues, turned outward. Their high leggings came up to the thigh and were embroidered with beads and bone ornaments. Outside of the garments mentioned they were absolutely bare, and when they bent over the middle of their anatomy was wholly uncovered.

I took my place at the head of the column to break trail. The Koksoak River was caught in the iron grasp of winter and we headed down its frozen surface. The going was good and we travelled at a fairly good pace.

At midday we drew up on the shore for a bite to eat. The meal over, we started right out again. I was feeling fine; my heart sang within me, and I tramped rapidly over the ice-covered river. The Indians followed more slowly and I left them farther and farther to the rear. A sharp bend in the river hid them from view altogether, but I tramped merrily on some distance ahead. The day was clear and my trail plain.

The river narrowed, running in spots between banks that gradually steepened. I became aware of the sound of rushing water beneath my feet. It became louder and louder, but it meant nothing to me.

I felt my snowshoes begin to sink through the icy crust. Directly ahead of me was a snow-covered block. I sensed that it was a rock and I jumped toward it. As I thrust myself upon it with a violent effort, the ice gave way altogether and my feet trailed in the water.

Mon Dieu! I was scared. I had been walking upon a thin crust of frozen spray covered with snow. My weight had broken through and sent the whole mass into the swirling waters of the rapids. I was marooned on a rock with barely space enough to sit down.

I was far ahead of the Indians and I cursed my impetuosity. I did not dare move and I waited, staring glumly at the rushing water. The cold crept into my bones and by the time my party came up I was chilled through and through.

The Indians had wisely taken to the shore and when they saw me perched on the rock, Ynish sang out:

"Whassa matter?"

He knew damned well what the trouble was; but I was so cold, and my teeth were chattering so, that I couldn't utter the curses that were in my heart.

Attaching a line to a stick of wood they cast it far out into the stream; it floated down on the far side of the rock and I grabbed it. Taking his axe, Ynish hewed down a convenient tree to which he had fastened the line. I pulled the tree toward me. It landed upstream a short ways and, caught by the rushing current, wedged its topmost branches against the rock. The shore end had already been anchored firmly and I walked across the crude bridge to the shore dryshod.

My experience taught me one lesson. Among the Indians the trail-breaker never travels without a staff; as he goes he taps the ice—tap, tap, tap. If the blows make a booming sound it is a sign that everything is well; but a dull sound is a sure warning of danger.

Above the rapids we took to the river again, and I stayed close to my companions. The weather was getting colder. Toward evening I made for the shore to fix a camp for the night. I had almost gained the shelter of the river-bank when the bottom dropped from beneath my feet. Down I plunged, but not into water.

When the water begins to recede, as the ice forms along the edges of the streams, a shelf of ice is left hanging in spots. I had stepped upon the thin crust and had fallen to the frozen river-bed. I was in an ice-trap. It was something like a cave; there was ice on all sides of me and just above my head was the little hole through which I had plunged.

My snowshoes were still on my feet, but I could not move. The Indians had seen me fall and they hurried up and pulled me out. Between the place where I had fallen and the shore there was a line of slush. In passing through it, I got wet to my knees and in no time at all my legs were frozen stiff.

Immediately the Indians started a fire, I stood before it and changed to dry clothes. The temperature was down around forty below zero, and stripping in that kind of weather is no joke. I caught a terrible cold.

In the morning I was so done in that I couldn't go on. Ynish examined me and he told me that what I needed was a good, big sweat.

"Sweat," I objected. "That's what's wrong with me. All I've been doing is sweating."

Without paying the least attention to my expostulations, Ynish set his men to building a little hut of willow. He built up a big fire and in it he placed large chunks of limestone. I began to strip in the little hut. Before I had finished, the chief and his men rolled in one of the rocks, white-hot, and it was followed in quick succession by others. It was like a Turkish bath.

I was in that hothouse for about an hour and I poured sweat. Then I went into a wigwam the Indians had built and they gave me a good hard rubbing. I went to sleep, and when I woke up the next morning I was as well as ever.

We travelled a hundred miles before we came to the bush country. After the bare lands around the post it seemed strange to me.

Not far from Lake Nichikeen, a limpid pool of water almost in the centre of the Labrador Peninsula, we passed Snowman Mountain. I wanted to visit it but my Indians would not go nearer than about twenty miles.

"Why won't you go with me?" I asked Ynish.

"In that mountain," he explained, "the snowman lives. Every year all of the animals that walk—the caribou, the marten, the mink—go there; and so do the birds. In the mountain they change and when they come out they have a new skin, one that is all white. The mountain is taboo to our people."

Try as I would, I could not budge them in their determination. The days were getting warmer and we waited for the ice around Nichikeen to break up. The

MY WOMAN WAITS

lake was a solid sheet of ice and as far as I could see it was going to remain so. I was in the wigwam one warm day when a distant call from lakeward drew me into the open.

"Uchimau, uchimau!" called Ynish. "The ice is going out!"

I hastened down to the shore. Except for a few cracks along the edge, the sheet of ice was as solid as ever; but as I watched the surface it began to shiver, rise up, and vanish. It was a most amazing sight; entirely different from the disappearance of ice on a stream.

The ice did not break up into floes, because there was nothing pushing upon it; but the whole surface seemed to waken into life. There was not a breath of air stirring but in a short time the ice had vanished and a wide expanse of crystal-clear water gleamed in the sunshine.

The Indians believe that the creations of nature have a spirit. Una, "the Spirit of Things", they believe causes the wonders of nature, and the transformation I had witnessed was one of the most marvellous.

With the water now open we took to canoes. We were heading for the East Main River and in between were many small lakes and streams. We crossed seventy-four portages, big and little, before we hit a little lake, Naokokah, I believe it was called, in the sucker country. The fishing was fine.

From the lake we headed overland on a brand-new trail bound for Lake Mistassini. At the head-waters of the lake we got canoes and paddled our way down the Waswanipi River to the lake of that name, where there was a post of the Hudson Bay Company.

It was our intention to go up the Nottaway River to Rupert House, but the factor told us that the river was booming and that travelling on it was apt to be a very dangerous proceeding. I consulted with Ynish and we decided not to risk it.

We started northward, heading for Namiscau. Between that place and Lake Mistassini we passed over the famous Portage of the Iroquois, where bleaching bones still mutely tell of the Indian massacre. The portage was three miles in length.

Soon after we passed the portage we came to a trading-post. We found a number of the Indian voyageurs who carry loads of goods and furs between the trading-posts and Rupert House.

"That man can portage the mountain," said Ynish, thus conveying that the Indian in question was the strongest man in the world.

"How much can he carry?" I asked, looking at the short, wiry figure with interest.

"Plenty," grunted Ynish. "Ask."

"You are a strong man?" I asked, turning to the man.

"Yes," he said, laughing.

"How much can you carry on your back, strapped?"

"Oh," he said readily. "Maybe six, seven sacks of flour."

"Those?" I asked, pointing to a stack of hundred-pound bags.

"Yes."

"Well," I said, "do it. I'll have to see you, before I believe you."

We walked over to the pile of bags. Tying two of the bags together, he bent down and put them across the back of his head, and at a word from him several of the Indians began to stack on five more. The fellow didn't even grunt under the load.

"Can you move with that load?" I asked in amazement.

Without deigning to answer, he started off at a slow, steady pace. He was followed by a little group. I was in the van and I expected him to wilt very quickly, but he had gone about a third of a mile without tiring.

"*Mon dieu,*" I cried. "That is enough."

I was running short of tobacco, but I felt that the strong man was deserving of a reward, and I gave him a pound of niggerhead. It was strong stuff, but I figured that it couldn't possibly hurt a man who could walk away with seven hundred pounds on his back.

Shortly after we reached Namiscau a heavy thunderstorm broke, and we had to stay over for a day longer than we expected to. Towards evening the storm blew away and, borrowing some nets, I went fishing. During the night we caught about two hundred sturgeon, mostly little ones. We let the small fry go and feasted on a couple of dozen of the biggest ones.

The Rupert River having subsided somewhat, we started down. This is one of the most spectacular rivers in the world. It is a series of rapids. We ran most of them, but when we came to the Four Steps, where the river dropped sheer in four places, spaced about a mile apart, we paused to marvel at the foaming, thundering, rushing water. I have seen nothing to equal it, excepting Niagara. Here we portaged our way around.

At Rupert House I had to wait for a boat to carry me to Moose Factory. It had been my intention to visit my good friend, Gaston Herodier, with my wife, before returning to "The Fort"; but while waiting for the boat he appeared at Rupert House, by great good luck.

I knew Herodier in Paris and we had a great get-together. He had been sent into the country east of Hudson Bay with two others to establish a trading-post. Soon after they had established themselves, his two men were drowned in an accident and he was left alone with the winter just started.

The Eskimos in that section were bad-hearted and when they came to the post and found him alone they got nasty. They had hung around the post for a week or

MY WOMAN WAITS

so, getting worse and worse, and one evening things came to a head. They got into his dwelling and demanded some goods. To smooth things over, Herodier argued with them, telling them that he must have furs in exchange for the goods.

"We will kill you," said the leader of the band.

From under their furs the Eskimos—there were about twenty of them—pulled knives. Herodier was cornered, but he did not lose his presence of mind. Realizing that courage always impresses a brave man, he just looked at them and, taking his cigar from his mouth, he smiled.

"Well," he said calmly, "suppose you kill me. What will happen? I will be dead. I will go to aurora borealis."

The Eskimos said nothing; they stirred restlessly under Herodier's keen glance. "And what will happen to you?" he went on, laughing. "When I am dead, I am dead; you will take the goods from here; but there will be no post here after that. What will happen? What will you do with your furs then? Ha, ha, ha; the joke will be on you."

The tables were turned. The Eskimos began to smile; they chuckled, they laughed; and Herodier laughed loudest and longest of all. That incident made my friend a power in his territory.

Herodier and I talked for a long while about old times, and then I continued on my way.

KABLUK OF THE ESKIMO

"Hello!" I roared, as I walked with a quick step to the familiar cabin at Moose Factory.

The tall figure of my soon-to-be father-in-law appeared. We shook hands in silence.

"The girl is in the kitchen," he said.

I found her with her arms bare, washing some clothes. I had made a long and almost desperate journey to fetch her away, but the North is no place for sentimental gushing. We stood with clasped hands, while I studied the simplicity of her dark eyes and the health of her tall, straight figure.

No need to tell of the ceremonies and festivities of a wedding. We were spliced with a firm, sure knot. Our feeling was that of old French Canada—one God, one country, one wife. There was a big dinner in the old Norwegian cabin, with music of an accordion, and singing and dancing. A few days later my wife wept many tears as she said good-bye to her people, and we left Moose Factory for Montreal, our first stop on the long trail to Ungava Bay and the old stamping-grounds of Akpek the chief.

At Montreal I talked with the officials of the company. Fort Ungava was growing in importance. New assistants were assigned to go north with me. I was to have under my command four men in all. The weeks we spent in Montreal were a kind of honeymoon, but still I found civilized life a burden, and wanted to get away to the North. So did my wife. She was eager to see her new home, although a log cabin in the land of the Midnight Sun might not seem any soft, luxurious new home for a bride.

"And," she told me, "I shall be curious to see your friend, Akpek the chief."

With the men recruited to be my assistants, we boarded the *Stord*. The voyage was uneventful, and presently the *Stord* was casting anchor in the river at Fort Ungava.

The first weeks of housekeeping are often the test for a young wife, and housekeeping at "The Fort" was no soft snap of a joke. I had expected my wife to bear the burden with a joyful will. She did. The North is no place for useless, indolent women. My wife pitched into the work with zest and zeal. She had had good training in the cabin of the old Norwegian at Moose Factory. She was as good a worker as an Eskimo squaw, and that is saying everything.

We were at breakfast, my wife and I, when there came a rap on the door. My wife rose to open it as the old woman who did the heavy work around the place was not in the room. I shook my head and nodded to her to keep her seat. Then I called:

"Come in."

The door swung open. "*Chimo*, my son," said Akpek, the chief.

I rose to my feet and my wife did likewise. The chief closed the door against the blustery weather and turned to us.

"*Chimo*, my father," I answered.

Akpek took his aged stone pipe from between his lips and puffed a cloud of blue smoke in a huge exhalation. It wreathed itself fantastically, and through it the aged patriarch's face took form.

"That is your woman?" he said, looking at my wife.

"Aha, my father," I responded, as my wife led him to a seat near the fire.

"That is good, my daughter," smiled Akpek.

"You will stay at the post, my father?" I asked.

"For two sleeps," he returned. "My woman waits for me at the village."

While we finished our meal he sat smiling placidly at us. From time to time he made a soft, clucking sound that seemed to come from deep within his barrel-shaped body.

"I wanted your man to take a woman from my tribe," he said finally to my wife, "but I was wrong."

In that way Akpek won his way into the good graces of my wife. Together we went over to the store.

CHAPTER XV

ANGEKOK AND THE CARIBOU

"Punalut", the berry month, passed rapidly away and the days began to grow shorter. Autumn weather prevailed. The grass turned from green to yellow and brown, and the weather became raw and dull.

High overhead disorderly flocks of birds passed on their way to the south, their discordant cries saying: "It is cold, it is cold, cold, cold, cold." Many of the flocks, pausing in their exodus to warmer climates, rested on the quiet waters.

The season for caribou hunting was approaching. I was invited to attend the annual caribou hunt of Akpek's tribe.

"I will be back in three months," I told my wife. "Meanwhile, you and Berthe look after things here at the post."

She nodded cheerfully. In the North a woman does not demand that a man be home every night. Nature among the snows does not tolerate small, mean selfishness.

Accompanied by Uyarak, who had brought the invitation, I journeyed to Akpek's village. Everyone was busy preparing for the caribou hunt and the approaching winter. The men fixed the sledges and their weapons, and the women put the finishing touches to the winter garments and sealskin boots.

Each day Akpek sent out young men to scout on the mainland for caribou signs, but it was still too early. The caribou is hunted at any time of the year, but especially in the autumn. Then the skin of the animal is free from parasites, the hair is short and firmly set.

Akpek called the elders of the tribe together to listen to the shaman; for through him the spirits would suggest the best way of taking advantage of the caribou migration.

The elders had gathered in Akpek's tent and we waited for the arrival of Tickek, the *angekok*. He came in his ceremonial garb and the chief at once opened the discussion. The magician sat silent as the elders offered the benefit of their mature experiences.

"The spirits speak," said the shaman, when they had finished. With grotesque contortions, he waved his magic stick until it pointed steadily toward one of the elders. He was immediately blindfolded and through his mouth came the questions asked of the spirits through their mouthpiece, the shaman.

"Will the herd be as large as the one last year?" asked the voice of the blindfolded one.

The magic stick wavered erratically for a moment;

ANGEKOK AND CARIBOU

its point dropped to the ground and inscribed three straight marks. The *angekok* stared at it solemnly.

"*Emarha*—maybe," he said.

Again the voice spoke. "Will the caribou travel in the usual direction?"

Again the stick described moved weirdly, marking cabalistic inscriptions which the *angekok* studied carefully, closely. The elders waited breathless for the answer to the momentous query. Akpek sat unmoved, the epitome of impassive dignity. The diviner, aware of his importance, murmured to himself in short, unintelligible snatches of mumbling sound.

"The caribou will come as usual," he predicted, in solemn tones. The elders stirred and murmured among themselves, but the *angekok* held up a warning hand for silence and continued: "But if any man violates a taboo the caribou will change his course."

With that he rose to his feet and left the council. At Akpek's suggestion, it was decided that the hunt should be conducted *en masse* instead of individually. Then men, united in a band, would drive the animals toward the stone enclosure on the mainland, where they would be butchered. The women were to remain at the village, keeping the dogs in check, ready to come across to attend to the hides when the hunt was over.

The days passed slowly. The scouts came and went, without bringing the awaited word. The tension in the village grew. Recalling the prophetic words of the shaman, the villagers spoke of broken taboos, and rumour had it that bows and arrows—land-animal weapons—had been found mixed with harpoons, narwhal spears, sea weapons, in the tent of a hunter.

Each day an umiak was transferred to the point of the island nearest to the mainland, ready for the prompt transport of hunting material; and the kayaks also were held in readiness. Each night the boats returned to the village cove.

One day I suggested to the chief that I would like to scout around with Uyarak and on the following morning the young hunter ferried me across to the main shore. Uyarak started out along a well-defined path. I called his attention to it and asked if he had been that way before. He said that he had.

"Which way did the other scouts go?" I queried.

Uyarak raised his hand and pointed in the same direction that the trail followed.

"Why did not they take the other direction?"

"The caribou, Kabluk," said Uyarak, "always come this way and not any other way. It is foolish to look for them where we never have seen them in the past."

"Let us try in the other direction," I said.

"It will be useless," retorted my companion. "The shaman has spoken."

"I shall go this way," I said, pointing to the east. "Will you come?"

Uyarak shrugged his shoulders. I took the lead

ANGEKOK AND CARIBOU

and he followed close behind. Through the day we travelled and when night fell we camped beside a little brook in a hollow, instead of returning to the village.

I could see that Uyarak was puzzled at my actions, but he said nothing and we went to sleep. Toward morning the temperature began to drop and I awoke chilled to the bone. Gathering together some moss, I asked Uyarak to light it with his flint. A peculiar vapour, like a light fog, was mounting up from behind the rocky ledge that hemmed us in. I stared at it.

Uyarak's eyes followed my gaze and his countenance changed in an instant to a picture of questioning surprise. Motioning to me to remain quiet, he dropped to his hands and knees and crawled cautiously up the bank of rough rock. He gave a short glance over the top and returned as carefully as he had gone.

"*Tuktu!*—Caribou!" he muttered; and without further explanation, he motioned to me to follow along a course parallel to the ridge, where we could walk upright without being seen by the grazing animals.

Half walking, half running, taking no time for food or rest, we hastened to carry the great news to the village. We reached the shore and Uyarak paddled us across to the island with a flashing stroke. Leaping to the beach, he mounted upon a high rock and, putting his cupped hand to his face, he shouted the magic message:

"*Tuktu!*—Caribou!"

KABLUK OF THE ESKIMO

The village was electrified. Men rushed to their tents for their hunting material; women ran around excitedly, the children laughed or cried, and the dogs howled in excitement.

We told our story. Tickek, the *angekok*, passed in and out among the villages, and as he went the people respectfully made way for him. He spoke loudly of broken taboos and hinted that a stranger to the Ighilik tribe had caused the herd to stray from its accustomed path. I saw that he was intimating that I was the cause, but he made no open accusation and I held my peace. Uyarak's belief in the magic of the shaman, however, had vanished, and he muttered his doubts openly.

"Beware, Uyarak," said an elder of the tribe warningly. "The spirits are powerful and the *angekok* speaks for them."

In a short time the men gathered around us at the beach, and Uyarak explained to the hunters that the vanguard of the herd had already passed to that west, and that we had come across the main body.

Akpek suggested that the whole body of hunters proceed to a distance of two hours' paddling along the southern shore, carrying as many of the youths of the village as they could ferry on their kayaks. From that point Uyarak and myself could locate the caribou herd and determine the direction of its leaders.

We set out, a flotilla of kayaks, and landed a silent, eager, primitive crowd. Akpek gave directions for the

Courtesy National Museum of Canada

THE MACHINE AGE IN ESKIMO LAND. AND THE OLD BOY IS A WIZARD WITH A BONE DRILL

ANGEKOK AND CARIBOU

hunt. It was important that a section of the herd be cut off and pushed toward the takim, a stone enclosure. The enclosure was by a deep lagoon of the ocean. On the lagoon the younger men and the eldest men in the party would wait in their kayaks for the arrival of the animals and prevent their escape seaward.

The chief assumed command of the kayaks. He bade Anotinoak, the tusked one, to direct the campaign by land. Anotinoak's group was composed of twelve of the bravest hunters of the tribe and a number of the younger men eager to make their names as warriors. Each of the hunters took his bow and arrows, his lance and knife.

Uyarak and I went by kayak to locate the caribou. The herd was moving northward. We paddled to a point on the coast where we expected to meet the head of the columns, landed, and scouted around. Mounting a huge boulder, we saw several caribou coming slowly toward us. Uyarak sucked in his breath sharply at the sight and let it hiss slowly from between clenched teeth as his avid eyes searched the horizon. Temptation was gnawing at his soul. The caribou, unless they changed their direction, would pass about two hundred paces from our position.

According to the arrangements, we should have let them pass unmolested, but the temptation was too great. Uyarak scanned the horizon carefully to make sure that the animals were really stragglers.

"All is well," he announced finally.

The land was barren of trees, but in the bottoms of the shallow ravines, where the caribou moved, dwarf willows grew. The animals came slowly toward us, feeding on soft moss that covered the ground.

"Come," said Uyarak.

The distance at which the animals would pass was too great for the range of our bows and, leaving our shelter, we walked diagonally, so that our presence would not frighten the caribou. As we neared their line of march we slowed our pace so that the unsuspecting animals would draw nearer to us.

"Aha," grunted Uyarak, as he darted into the shelter of a huge boulder. I glanced over my shoulder. Uyarak was fitting an arrow into his bow-string. The caribou came steadily on. When they were within easy bowshot, Uyarak uttered a plaintive cry.

"I am sorry that I have to kill you," he wailed, giving the customary warning, without which the Eskimo considers it unfair to kill.

The startled animals threw up their heads at the unusual sound, but before they could turn, Uyarak had loosed his first missile.

One of the caribou dropped with an arrow through its heart, and the other two bounded away. Before they were out of range Uyarak loosed another arrow, wounding one of the fleeing animals in the thigh and disabling it. The other one got away.

ANGEKOK AND CARIBOU

At a signal from Uyarak I ran after the wounded animal and drove my lance into its side. We dragged the two carcasses to the boulder, in order to be able to locate them later, and continued scouting for the main herd.

For an hour we pushed to the west, often climbing high rocks to get wider views of the terrain. Occasionally Uyarak dropped to the ground and listened for the sound of distant hoofs.

Finally, topping a slight rise, we sighted an immense dark mass, a dim, dusky ocean of moving forms. It was the main body of caribou. It was to the south of our position, so thick and extended that it was impossible to discern its actual limits. As far as I could see the ground was a heaving dark-brown mass, with myriads of interspersed white spots, topped by thousands and thousands of antlers that tossed like willows on shifting soil.

Now that we had discovered the herd it was our job to survey it and locate the weak point where it could be split in two. The caribou are not keen of sight, but their sense of smell is strongly developed and we were careful to march upwind.

Hour after hour we marched along the vast length of the herd without seeing an end of it. At last, tired and hungry, we decided to return to the kill we had made earlier in the day and remain there until the next morning.

It was late when we reached the boulder that marked

the spot. Yuarak was afraid to light a fire so near the herd, and we decided to move several miles to the north and camp for the night. Uyarak deftly butchered our kill and we feasted on tender venison steaks roasted on pieces of willow.

We were up before dawn the next day. The light of the rising sun was beginning to show in the heavens, a yellow sheet of luminescence that grew higher and brighter as we advanced. We journeyed fast to rejoin the main body of the hunters. Akpek stood silent until Uyarak had finished his recital. With quick, terse sentences the chief planned the campaign. Anotinoak and his men were to penetrate the herd, cutting it in two and driving one section to the southern shore of the lagoon.

The chief and his party were to remain at the head of the lagoon, ready to board their kayaks as soon as the animals took to the water.

The details of the hunt settled, the land party started toward the south. Uyarak and I went along. As we neared the herd, a reverberating rumble warned us that the animals were on the move. Topping a slight rise, we came upon a magnificent sight. As far as the eye could see the earth was covered with a mass of hair backs over which a thick vapour from the breathing animals swirled; and the sound of myriad hoofs drumming on the hard ground filled the heavens.

Anotinoak, the tusked one, led his warriors into the fray. His voice rose in the shrill, plaintive cry of

ANGEKOK AND CARIBOU

the hunter who is about to kill. With a wild series of shouts we charged down the slope, loosing our arrows into the compact mass of sweating, heaving bodies. The caribou, terror-stricken, jostled and crushed each other in vain attempts to escape the danger that beset them. Their very numbers, a protection against the attacks of beasts of prey, rendered them helpless before the superior intelligence of man, their most dreaded enemy.

Shooting at random, it was impossible to miss the compact mass. We reached the fringe of the herd. Without pausing, the hunters began slashing at their victims with their knives, lunging with their wicked spears, cutting a wide swath of death.

The human wedge moved into the dense mass slowly and with great difficulty. On the left were the animals that were to escape the hunters; on the right the victims that Anotinoak had marked for destruction. We advanced farther and farther. The drove of living beasts were inexorably separated by fallen carcasses into two distinct groups.

At last the hunters had cut off a vast living triangle of frightened beasts and were beginning to press it toward the north. Having turned the lead animals to the north, the great drive went forward of its own volition, pushed on by the rush of the terror-stricken caribou in the rear.

The movement to the north started slowly. Quickly

KABLUK OF THE ESKIMO

increasing its speed, the mass of animals, thousands upon thousands, stampeded madly toward the lagoon, which was to be the butchering place where Akpek and his hunters could do their work of slaughter.

The mad stampede whirled on like a tornado. A thick cloud of choking dust hid the herd from our view, and all sounds were drowned out by the roar of myriads of hoofs beating the hard ground. They thundered on, an irresistible force sweeping everything from its path.

The tusked one and his men, once the caribou were under way, ran at top speed along one side of the herd, toward the lagoon. I followed more leisurely with Uyarak. I was amazed to see the herd slowing down. As we came to the lagoon the reason was plain.

Near the water's edge was a fence made of hundreds of small cairns placed some ten feet apart and extending in a convex line for almost a mile. From a distance the cairns resembled the silhouettes of men. The leaders of the caribou hesitated in the face of this new menace. Those in the rear pressed in upon them impatiently. The flight of the herd was checked.

Anotinoak and his men were upon them again and the bloody carnage was renewed. Under the unrelenting attack of the hunters the caribou fell by the score, and in falling their bodies sent a ripple of movement through the mass.

In spite of the resistance of the front ranks, the

ANGEKOK AND CARIBOU

pressure of the herd slowly forced the head of the column on to the line of cairns. The leaders were thrust through the spaces between the cairns and the bulk of the herd passed through. Anotinoak and his men hung behind them like wolves, slaying, slaying. A rampart of dead and dying caribou, slippery with blood, hindered the movements of the Eskimos. The remnant of the herd, having passed the cairns, straggled on toward the lagoon. There were still thousands of them.

Fatigued with their exertions, hoarse with shouting and satiated with unceasing butchery, Anotinoak and his men paused to rest. Accompanied by Uyarak, I went at a dog-trot to the north where, at the edge of the water, Akpek and his men were awaiting the last act of the hunt.

We came upon the youngsters, who lined the side-shores of the lagoon to prevent the escape of the caribou to the landward. Akpek and the main band of his hunters were at the northern end of the headland.

We heard a sound of a prodigious splashing. Calling upon me to follow, Uyarak ran toward an eminence that overlooked the lagoon. An amazing scene lay before our eyes.

The front ranks of the caribou were taking to the water, and in dense ranks the others followed, lashing the water into foam, and making the air resound with the muffled trampling of hoofs on the pebbly bottom and the clashing of disturbed stones.

Ploughing a wide furrow in the still water, the

leading caribou swam without apparent agitation. After them a mass of dark backs continued to flow over the shore's edge into the churned water, until the lagoon was half covered with anxious heads over which a forest of antlers waved.

"A-ya, a-ya!" From the north came a distant call that was echoed and re-echoed from all sides. Turning, I saw the kayaks glide silently out over the water in a long-drawn line that allowed each hunter ample room for action.

At the shrill yell of the Eskimos the leaders of the swimming herd tried to turn back, but the pressure from the rear forced them on. Some turned toward the sides of the trap, but along the lateral shores the Eskimo boys were lined, who, with blood-curdling shrieks and yells, emulated the vocal exercises of their elders with gusto. And the antlered swimmers turned back upon the splashing, milling herd.

Into the midst of the bewildered caribou swept the kayaks of the hunters. The Eskimo lances stabbed, stabbed, stabbed. The men slew as rapidly as they could plunge their keen, slender weapons into unresisting backs and sides. In the frightful and confused turmoil, the affray degenerated into a pitiful butchery. It sickened me.

The lagoon was a bloody froth, covered with the floating carcasses of the victims. The wild splashing and the plaintive bleating of dying animals made a

ANGEKOK AND CARIBOU

ghastly concert. The caribou were hunted down to the last animal until at last a deathlike silence brooded over the scene of the slaughter.

With the approach of darkness, Anotinoak and his men came up. Fires were lighted, illuminating the place of death with spectral light. Tired out, I threw myself down to sleep. Akpek and his men did likewise, for on the morrow there was much work to be done.

We were up with the dawn. With Uyarak I went down to the shore where his kayak lay. We were to carry a message to the village. I did not feel much like talking, but there was something in my companion's manner that made me wonder.

"What is the matter, Uyarak?" I asked. "Are you not pleased with the hunt?"

"Aha, yes," he answered in a serious tone. "It is not that."

"What is it?" I pressed him.

"It is you," he explained, "your magic. You found the caribou in a place where they never were before. It has made my people wonder."

"Aha!"

"Kabluk," he went on respectfully, "your spirit is indeed a great one."

Uyarak paddled fast. I lay behind him on the top of the kayak. We arrived at the island. The whole village, women, children, and dogs, lined the shore.

Not a voice was raised in inquiry as to the success of the hunt.

As he stepped ashore, Uyarak quietly announced that the chief had ordered the camp moved across to the mainland. That was all. Not a word was said regarding caribou; but everybody knew that the camp would not have been ordered shifted had not the hunt been successful. The message meant that it was easier to go to the kill than to bring the carcasses to the village.

We walked up to the tents in silence, except for the yapping of the dogs. The women began to chatter and laugh and one, more curious than her sisters, asked if caribou had been seen.

"Aha," returned Uyarak casually.

"Were any killed?" queried another.

"Aha," said my companion again. It was enough. The women immediately set to work knocking down the tents, packing the camp gear, and getting the umiaks ready for the trip across the channel.

In a continuous stream they carried load after load to the shore, until everything was piled in the women's boats. The dogs went aboard next and the party shoved off. The fleet was made up of ten umiaks. It advanced slowly under the impulse of the oars.

It presented an amusing sight. The women rowers pulled haphazardly, without timing or rhythm; and a confusion of voices, laughter, and the yelping of the dogs

ANGEKOK AND CARIBOU

could be heard afar. Uyarak and I, in our dignified, masculine kayak, navigated at the head of the flotilla.

For a while a little breeze allowed the women to use their sails, but it soon faded away and they took to the paddles again. Towards evening we were abreast the lagoon and Uyarak paddled for the shore. The squadron of noisy, ridiculous umiaks followed. Close to a small stream the women put up their tents, and the umiaks were hauled out of the water and turned bottoms up.

Leaving the women to their work, Uyarak took me over to the edge of the lagoon. A group under Anotinoak were busily at work and my companion joined them at their labours.

I watched their skilful hands preparing the carcasses. A quick slitting of the skin in the centre of the under body and along the legs is done with a double-edged fleshing knife; the entrails are removed; the head and marrow bones severed; and the body cut up in a masterful manner.

Anotinoak, the tusked one, paused now and again to snatch a titbit with hands dripping with blood and eat it. Each of the hunters had killed an average of one hundred animals, and rapid as the men were in disposing of the bodies, there still remained at least four days of hard work for everybody before the transporting of the kill to the new village could begin.

I wandered over the field of carnage, seeking Akpek, whom I found hard at work near the barrier of cairns.

KABLUK OF THE ESKIMO

Darkness was near. He knocked off work when I came up. I guided him to the new village.

The transfer of the tons of caribou flesh to a point near the village, where the meat was dried upon high poles, took all of a week. During that time sledging parties were sent over the thick moss to locate isolated carcasses of victims that had strayed away to die. Many of them had been half eaten by wild animals and for a long time wolves prowled the vicinity.

In the village there was much laughter and feasting. The caribou hunt had been a great success.

CHAPTER XVI

ANOTINOAK, THE TUSKED ONE, AND HIS BATTLE WITH THE WOLVES

AFTER weeks of fine weather at Akpek's village the sky became overcast with heavy, dull grey clouds. A diffused light pierced the deep opaque curtain with difficulty, spreading a dim gloom around. All nature seemed to brood; the air was heavy and uneasy; there was not a breath of wind.

Toward evening a breeze from the north began to stir the curtain of cloud. It increased in force and speed. Instantaneously the whole country disappeared in a blanket of driven snow. Blown by the howling gale, the snow, beating and biting one's flesh with teeth of bitter sharpness, drifted over the bare lands of the North, entombing everything under a shroud of virgin white.

For three days the blizzard raged. It was impossible to go out of the tents. Under the pressure of the storm the snow was thrown almost horizontally, and it was as hard and cold as hail; it levelled the terrain to a uniform sheet of dazzling whiteness and drifted in through all apertures, no matter how small. The howling wind shook the tents threateningly, but the storm had been expected, and everything had been securely braced.

About noon on the third day the snow ceased to fall; the clouds broke up, showing patches of dull blue sky; the wind died down. In its wake the storm left two feet of hard-packed snow; winter had arrived. The task of uncovering the snow-hidden objects was not an easy one.

Several days of steady work were required to bring the camp to its normal state; and before the snow hardened suitably for the building of the igloos, a wall of snow, several feet high, was built up around the encampment to cut the icy wind.

Akpek and his people were delighted with the change in the weather. The channel separating their island home from the mainland was slowly but perceptibly narrowing; each night the shore-ice extended farther out. The snow that had fallen into the water rendered it sluggish, thick, and slushy; and one cold, calm night was sufficient to bridge the channel over. Every brook, creek and river was ice-sheeted, as were also the swamps and lakes.

Myriads of snowbirds, fat and white, had come with the snow, and the children had a great time netting them. They were a welcome change of diet to the Eskimos, and Akpek ate as many as twenty of the plump morsels at a meal.

The air was brisk and invigorating; the sky took

ANOTINOAK AND HIS BATTLE

on a more pallid tinge during the hours of daylight; and the nights became darker, longer, and colder.

The villagers busied themselves cutting and drying meat, preparing the hides, working over their sledges, fixing the dog harness, and getting ready for the winter travelling.

For some days after the big storm the men tested the nature of the snow banks with long rods, trying its consistency by stamping on it. All were anxious to build their igloos, but the snow was not suitable for the purpose. To be of the proper consistency, it must give out a sound like that of a hollow tree tapped by a fist.

When the men did begin the construction of the snow-houses, I worked beside Uyarak. With ivory snow knives we cut out rectangular blocks about three feet long, two feet wide, and half an inch thick. We placed a first tier in a circle about thirty feet in diameter with the tops of the blocks leaning slightly inward, and cemented the interstices with loose snow.

Each layer we inclined more and more toward the centre of the igloo. To facilitate the sloping of the upper part, we sliced the sides of the upper blocks to fit. Uyarak carved the top block, the keystone of the structure, to fit exactly, and I helped him put it in place. The structure was finished. Secondary lean-tos were erected near by.

Inside the igloo, an excavation covering about

half of the floor space was cut out in blocks, and the sections were used to build up a platform upon which skins were piled to form sleeping-places. In the front part of the snow-house a tall man could stand erect, but at the rear the height of the walls decreased proportionately.

The main entrance to the dwelling was a low tunnel, leading to a small chamber reserved for cooking; from there another low entrance led to the main chamber. From it the outhouses could be reached.

Willow twigs served as an insulator between the snow-platform and the skins which formed the beds. On a smaller side-platform stood a stone lamp, with its wick swimming in oil. Lines for drying clothing stretched from one side of the chamber to the other. It was very bright in the interior of the igloo and quite warm, the temperature remaining a degree or so above the freezing point, no matter how cold it was outside.

In a few days the appearance of the village had changed completely and an immaculate collection of white domes, glittering in the sun, graced the encampment. Each family had selected a convenient spot and erected dwellings suited to their needs.

The snow-houses absorbed all sound. From without, the village was usually a city of the silent; within, little or nothing of the outdoor activities could be heard.

Akpek wanted to push on to the western end of Hudson Straits to meet a member of the tribe who

ANOTINOAK AND HIS BATTLE

had gone to Baffin Land to hunt the musk ox. Now that everything for the winter months had been prepared in the village, he made ready to depart.

Four or five of his kinsmen and their families were going along, as were a few of his friends; and provisions were made for a long, arduous journey.

Akpek had the best dog-team in the village. His huskies were fierce brutes standing fully thirty inches high, offspring of a dam that had been allowed to mate with a timber wolf. The team was made up of nine males, led by a magnificent female. Two years old, they feared nothing but the voice and whip of their master, and the chief kept them in hand by an iron rule.

During the summer, no work being required of them, Akpek permitted them to run loose on the island, where they foraged around for food. On the mainland they were kept in leash. I looked at their gaunt bodies with a feeling akin to pity.

"Fat dogs cannot pull *komutiks*," said Akpek, catching my eye. "Heavy dogs break through the snow crust."

The dogs passed one another with distrust. Stiff-legged, with necks outstretched and short ears pricked up, they glared sideways at each other. Deep growls emphasized the threat of their slavering chops and long, uncovered fangs.

Two of the dogs, enemies of long standing, watched

each other from the corners of their eyes; thick manes bristled, and throaty growls changed into fierce snarls each time they drew breath.

One of the belligerents made a slight move. Instantly his antagonist charged at him like a flash, head held high and terrible teeth gleaming. Down they went; a whirl of entangled, threshing bodies sent the snow swirling upward; hair flew and foam splashed from the gnashing jaws of the combatants.

Upright on to their hind legs they surged. With forepaws upon each other's shoulders they challenged each other with bloodshot eyes. Snapping savagely with crimson-stained jaws they went down again, mouthing palpitating flesh, which muffled their unearthly growls.

The cruel teeth of one of the dogs struck home. A shrill yell of pain announced the finish of the battle. Rising on three legs the vanquished, his back curved high and his head hanging, dragged himself away to the side of an igloo, where he squatted, licking a badly torn leg.

The victor shook his head and sneezed energetically; with bared fangs and stiff legs he slowly followed after his victim. Squatting near by, he gave vent to a howl of victory. It was a challenge to the world. Nothing happened and, opening his great mouth in a contemptuous yawn, he fell to licking his wounds.

I could not understand why the men made no

ANOTINOAK AND HIS BATTLE

effort to stop the carnage. Many of them had gone on with their work during the battle as though it was an ordinary occurrence; among them was Akpek, who was busy placing a bit of ivory runner on his sledge. I mentioned the matter to him.

"Did you notice the other dogs?" he asked.

"No, my father."

"They did not interfere."

"Why?" I asked thoughtfully.

"Among dogs," he answered, smiling, "as among men, there must be a chief. Among my people the head-man is supreme until he is supplanted or dies; among the dogs the strongest must also maintain his leadership. With them it is in bloody contest."

"Is the fight necessary?" I asked, looking at the whipped dog.

"It is," the chief answered. "Until the best dog has won decisively over the others, he cannot become a leader among them. Even the other dogs recognized the importance of the fight."

"And if you stopped them . . ."

"Had we stopped them, it would have been renewed over and over until a final decision was reached. Now it is settled."

And the chief pointed at the king of the team. He had stopped licking his wounds and with an air of boredom was receiving the adulation of the females and the flattering respect of the males.

KABLUK OF THE ESKIMO

Before sleeping-time came the party was in readiness for an early departure in the morning. The day dawned clear, with a crispy tang in the air. The dogs were eager to be on the move, and with Akpek's team in the lead we dashed on our way.

That night we camped in a willow thicket near a frozen stream. Outside it was bitterly cold, but in the hastily erected igloos we were comfortable. We had passed many wolf tracks on the day's journey, and they all pointed toward the place where the caribou slaughter had taken place. I remarked that it was strange that we had not heard the howl of wolves.

"*Amorok* does not cry on a full belly," said Akpek sagely.

"Aha," grunted Anotinoak, the tusked one, approvingly.

"The grey beast is bad when he is hungry," commented Uyarak.

"Aha," grunted the tusked one again. "I remember once . . ."

He paused and drew thoughtfully on his pipe, continuing: "It was five winters ago. This man was travelling with his son, Uluk, who was then a boy of ten, many sleeps to the west.

"We noticed the tracks of various animals in our path. Among them were prints of *amorok*, the great grey wolf. We tramped along the deserted tundra, our eyes open for game, our bows ready for action.

ANOTINOAK AND HIS BATTLE

"The sun was beginning to hide behind the distant hills when Uluk placed his hand warningly upon my arm. He pursed his lips toward the east. This man saw a huge wolf prowling behind the boulders which were abundant on the tundra in that vicinity.

"Soon another appeared on the other side, skulking behind the rocks. There were no signs of them in the direction we were going. We moved faster in order to gain our igloo before the sun disappeared altogether.

"Night came. With the darkness the snow began to fall, hiding all tracks. The wind moaned low as it passed over the boulders; it did not drown out the distant howl of *amorok*, the great grey wolf. It was answered in quick succession from all directions.

"The wolf pack was gathering. This man knew that *amorok* was hungry enough to make the most cowardly members of the pack fierce and bold aggressors. And this man knew that his igloo was too far away to reach before the pack closed in. The howls grew louder and we sighted stray forms through the curtain of falling snow.

"At a little distance from us there was a gigantic mass of stone with sheer sides. 'Come,' this man cried to his son. And together we ran for that haven. The phantom-like forms were increasing.

"Giving Uluk a line, this man lifted him upon his shoulder, and, lifting him by the feet, he pushed the boy up to the full extent of his upthrust arms.

KABLUK OF THE ESKIMO

Uluk got a firm footing in a notch of the rock and threw the line over the top, as though he was cracking a whip. The line wrapped itself around a projection at the top and it held firmly.

"Uluk climbed to the top of the boulder and I sent up our equipment. I waited for the line to come down with my back against the rock, knife in hand.

"Through the blown snowflakes, I caught the baleful gleam of many eyes. *Amorok*, the great grey wolf, wise to our action, was closing the circle. The line came down and I went up hand over hand—quickly.

"The faint glow in the west vanished. The sun had gone down. We waited in the darkness, on the alert. With the deepening of the night the snow ceased to fall.

"Scores of gleaming eyes surrounded us. Now and then there came an ominous call. Out of the night the pin-points of light winked as the animals crept nearer.

"We were besieged. There was not much room on the rock. The night was cold. My son was not frightened but he shivered on our icy perch. Seeing that he was tired and sleepy, this man told him to lie down and sleep.

"Between us we had about twenty arrows, but those of my son were small. Behind every stone there crouched a beast. The wolves kept tightening their circle and their yelps were increased tenfold by the echoes from the rocks. This man felt that the boulder was a safe refuge.

"*Amorok* was very hungry. Throwing aside all caution, the hunger-maddened animals hurled themselves at the barrier that protected us. There rose a dreadful yell from hundreds of wicked throats. The scraping of feet on the ice and the sharp clawing on the rock warned this man that the brutes were trying to reach the top. This man could see them; long, gaunt, grey-furred bodies that leaped onward with devilish eyes and snarling mouths. Time and again they sprang, straining for a firm foothold, only to slip and fall to the foot of our refuge.

"The howls of pain that followed told their own story; the wolves were devouring the injured among them. The howls of the pack, the shrieks of the victims, the voice of the wind, all seemed to unite in a vast tumult that would make the bravest fear. At my feet my boy slept, unaware of his hard bed, the bitter cold, the fearful noise.

"At last the light of morning began to creep leisurely over the eastern horizon. At my very feet, it seemed, there were an unaccountable number of savage brutes squatted, with wicked heads upturned, mouths wide open, and lolling tongues; a maze of awesome beasts, cold snouts, rumbling growls emerging from the surrounding shadows.

"Now that they could see their prey, *amorok* roused

to fresh efforts. Struggling to reach us, leaping and clawing, the wolves dropped into the open jaws of their fellows, and their blood stained the snow scarlet.

"Uluk awakened at the clamour. Now that we could see, we fitted arrows to our bows and shot into the densely packed, shifting mass below us. Every arrow pierced a body, a panting, quivering carcass that was immediately seized upon and devoured. We continued to shoot our arrows.

"All through the morning the survivors of the pack ate of the fare we provided. Their hunger appeased at last, the wolves, a few at a time, grew timid and retreated. Before the sun had travelled much higher, the pack had melted away.

"The snow was slushy with blood, and nothing but clean-picked bones were left to remind us of our experience.

"I have spoken," Anotinoak finished, and he resumed his reclining position on his soft deerskin hides.

"Aha," said Akpek. "Now we will sleep."

We were up with the dawn, heading north-westward. It took the party a little more than two weeks to reach the Payne River. The stream was frozen solid and we got to the other side without trouble. A broken sledge compelled a halt several days later and a camp was put up.

The weather remained uniformly good and several hunting parties were sent out to look for game. Kopeak

Courtesy National Museum of Canada

OFF FOR A SUMMER RESORT, AND THE LORD OF THE IGLOO PREPARES HIS LADY FOR THE OUTING

ANOTINOAK AND HIS BATTLE

brought in a caribou he happened to come upon and Uyarak reported signs of fox in the willow thickets to the west.

That night Uyarak mentioned that he had seen many ptarmigan in the neighbourhood of a small lake, dazed with the cold. He had even walked in among them without exciting them, knocking a number of them over with the handle of his whip. That reminded Akpek of an experience of earlier days.

"In my youth," said the chief, "I saw a sight that few men see.

"A wolf drew near my igloo one night. At last he came into the entrance where the dogs were. Seizing one, he carried it away, leaving its mates cowering.

"I ran out with my lance. I could hear the yelps of agony of my dog and I started in that direction. *Amorok* dropped his dying victim and fled.

"Knowing that the thief would come back for his kill, I made camp in a thicket of willows close by. It was a very cold, calm night, and this man lay awake, listening to the loud reports of the ice snapping apart in the intense cold.

"Tired and cold, I could not sleep; but apart from the vapour that came from my mouth when I breathed, I lay as lifeless as the frigid snow, the motionless air, the dreary willows.

"I drowsed off. I was awakened by the rapid flutter of speedy wings and a flock of ptarmigan dropped toward the grove of willows. A flock of twice twenty of the birds landed on the snow.

" 'Ka ka ka ka ka' called each ptarmigan, as it came to rest in a tiny glade. Daylight was just scattering the shades of night but I could see their pink eyes plainly.

"The birds stood motionless for a time; their feathers bristled rigidly. It seemed as though they were waiting tensely for some kind of a signal.

"Just as the pallid rays of the rising sun fell upon the glade, a ptarmigan moved to the centre of the small clearing. Its wings were spread and it moved on stiff legs. Walking solemnly, as if commencing the prelude of some strange dance, it strutted into an ungainly sort of rhythm.

"At that the whole gathering rose, wings outstretched and hanging low, feathers bristling, and legs held stiffly, forming a circle around the leader.

"The central figure of the scene flapped his wings on the hard snow. It sounded like the beat of a primitive drum. Boom! Boom! Slowly at first it went, accelerating into a weird cadence; and with each beat it stepped a pace to one side.

" 'Kak!' called the leader; and 'Boom!' went his wings.

"In time with the drumming of the leader, the other ptarmigan leaped sideways, giving a slight flap of their extended wings. 'Kak! Boom! Kak!

ANOTINOAK AND HIS BATTLE

Boom!' The birds danced as one, circling in an endless single file.

"The boom of the leader's wings increased in volume, the calls more frequent, and the interval between beats diminished as the dance proceeded.

"The snow, beaten violently by the wings of the dancers, flew like dust under the feet of a running deer. Round and round the white-feathered file went, speeding up its pace until the clearing resounded with the clamour.

"The ptarmigan leader broke the measure suddenly. The dance was over. The flock flew away. The dance was over."

So Akpek's tale ended.

CHAPTER XVII

A MESSENGER FROM THE LAND OF THE MUSK OX

WE reached the great northern sea late in November, and camp was made at the southern end of a deep inlet. The country was fine for trapping, fox signs being abundant. Uyarak and I worked together and he taught me to make traps.

"When you get by the high bluff at the end of the creek," he explained, "you will find many flat stones. Make a house of them, leaving only a small opening at the top.

"Place your bait inside, and *treganeak*, the fox, will jump in for it. He cannot get out. The opening will be too small."

A week passed without a sign of the Eskimos we had come to meet. There was much hunting and fishing.

With Uyarak, I went often to examine the traps. We had many of them on the sea ice. It was easy to set deadfalls there. Great slabs of ice were plentiful and we used them for the walls. The bait was so arranged that a slight pull on it dropped the heavy mass on the victim.

A MESSENGER

One day we had an especially good bag. Returning to the camp, I handed the pelts to Nayume and, turning to Akpek, I asked:

"Are foxes numerous, as a rule, my father?"

"Every four or five dips of the sun," said Akpek gravely, "the fox is more abundant. The following season they die."

"Why?"

"The mice on which the foxes feed begin to die off," the chief explained, "and *treganeak* becomes insane. He moves with shivering legs, his tongue blackens, he falls, dies. All over the country dead foxes can be found."

I puffed slowly on my pipe, gazing thoughtfully at the patriarch. "What is the cause?"

The old man shrugged his shoulders. "It is not known," he said, "but I have noticed that when the foxes sicken, so too do our dogs. My people also do not feel well."

"But there must be a cause for this pestilence," I insisted.

"Aha, my son. Evil spirits enter every living body. Even the sun looks queer and the weather is bad."

"Does the sun cause the trouble?"

"*Emarha, emarha,*" the chief said sadly, "—maybe."

Gloomy December, "when the sun goes down", passed slowly by. In the inlet little driftwood was to be found and scouting parties were sent up and down the coast. It was the time of the great darkness and they did not dare venture very far from the camp; our supply of firewood dwindled.

One night the wind rose with terrific force. With it came an unexpected rise in the temperature. The earth trembled and the wind howled in terrorizing fury; its loud shrieking drowning out all sounds. At intervals, thumps against the walls of the igloo told of objects torn loose by the wind and carried on its wings like wisps of straw. After a particularly hard bump, Akpek shouted for me to go out and see if our belongings were all right.

I crawled out through the tunnel-like passage. Outside, I got to my feet, but I had not taken three steps when the wind caught me, throwing me in its fury flat upon the ground. It was so strong that I could not get up, and I had to drag myself on my belly back to the entrance of the igloo.

The hurricane lasted but half an hour, but in that short time it wrought terrible havoc. With its passing the temperature began to drop, drop, drop.

"Never in my long life," commented Akpek, "have I seen a wind as strong as that. The spirits of the air are angry, surely."

The following morning was spent in searching for belongings that had been blown away. Many of the articles, objects that had cost their owners

A MESSENGER

much labour to procure or fashion, were hopelessly wrecked.

The hurricane had swept a deep path through the snow, wrecking every snow-wall in the village that stood without the usual curve. At spots the earth was bare of snow; at others the snow was piled up in tremendous banks.

That night we were talking of the storm and the destruction it had wrought. I mentioned how it had flattened me to the ground.

"Aha," said old Nayume. "It is terrible to be caught outside when the spirits of the air are angry.

"Many years ago there was a family travelling far to the west. The mother rode on the *komutik*. The father and daughter ran beside it. The girl was almost a grown woman.

"They were not far from the place where they were going and it was snowing. The curtain of white hid from them the warning storm-clouds which were rushing their way.

"The dogs only knew what was coming and they were frightened. Their behaviour made the man uneasy. He turned to call to his daughter but at that moment the hurricane struck with a terrible shriek.

"The small lake they were travelling over was packed deep with snow, but in a few moments it was swept into the air. Behind there was nothing but clear ice.

"The man and his wife clung to the sledge, and the

dogs clawed frantically at the slippery ice, but their efforts were as nothing under the impulse of the storm. They slid sideways as the speed increased. They came to the edge of the shore, where they hit with a terrific crash.

"Arising, the parents missed their daughter. Receiving no answer to their calls, they hastily erected a snow-shelter and cowered behind it until the storm finally blew away. In the wake of the storm snow came and it was not until the next morning that they could begin the search.

"For many long dreary hours they hunted. At last they found the body of the girl seated against a huge boulder where the wind had blown her. Her head rested upon her hands and she seemed to be sleeping.

"The mother called to her softly. She did not answer. The father touched her arm. A chill went through him. The body, an icy statue, toppled sideways. The cold fingers of frozen death had rigidly set her in position for her last slumber."

There was still much work to be done, and the days that followed the hurricane became very cold. Everything touched with the bare hand clung to the skin as though glued and the touch of metal burned like fire. The meat had to be chopped with an axe, the seal oil was as thick as tallow.

The dogs had to gnaw determinedly to mouth the frozen flesh. They were not given water to drink,

FINALLY THE BLIZZARD PASSED. IN ITS WAKE IT LEFT A WORLD OF IMMACULATE WHITE, WITH HUGE SNOW DRIFTS

A MESSENGER

so they quenched their thirst by licking the snow; and when they slept they curled themselves up on the bare snow.

Soon most of the traces of the hurricane disappeared; but one feature remained. The wind had blown away most of the firewood; there was hardly any driftwood along the coast, because of the strong currents, and we were without fire.

We had plenty of food but we had to eat it raw. We lived on sea food, mostly salmon. There was little to do. We were confined in the village limits during the long boreal night, and that left us with too much leisure on our hands.

Each day Akpek sent parties along the shore in quest of wood and the leaders had instructions to keep their eyes open for signs of the people we were expecting. Day after day the parties went out and returned without material results.

Tiring of our diet of sea food, I suggested to Uyarak one day that we go inland in search of deer or bear. We hunted for three days but game had vanished. Even the foxes were scarce.

"Too cold," said Uyarak succinctly.

At the village, the men, unable to hunt, hung around aimlessly; they ate, they talked, they gambled; and at times they merely sat with vacant eyes and blank minds. The women had their usual household tasks to do and they remained their cheerful selves.

KABLUK OF THE ESKIMO

Toward the end of the month, when the world seemed at its darkest, snow started to fall heavily. About noon a high wind from the west sprang up with a suddenness equalled only by its force. With insensate rage it whirled over the bleak tundra. It was the beginnings of a blizzard. The gale increased in its might. The whipping snow was terrible to face and for three days the storm continued without a lull. None of the villagers ventured forth.

Finally the blizzard passed. In its wake it left a world of immaculate white with huge snowdrifts. In the open spaces the wind had lashed the snowy surface, giving it the appearance of a tumultuous sea frozen into quiescence.

That night I walked forth with Akpek. The old chief remarked that the blizzard had entirely changed the appearance of the country and that it would be difficult to find one's bearings. Smiling gravely, he pointed to the sky and said:

"To find the road we must look in the sky, my son."

"Aha," I answered.

"There is our guide," he continued, pointing to the North star. " 'The star that never moves.' "

I nodded and he went on to point out the Big Dipper, which he called "The Reindeer Stars", and the Little Dipper, which was known as "The Shortrib Stars".

"*Ukiok*, the winter, will soon be going," he said at last, and we turned back to his igloo.

A MESSENGER

As the days passed, the pallid glow on the eastern horizon changed to a dull light and the sun's rays shot up vertically into the sky. By degrees the rays inclined downward and one noon the upper edge of the cheering orb of the sun grazed the horizon, putting an end to the interminable night.

Men and beasts roused themselves as though awakening from a long sleep. Filling our lungs with invigorating air and eyeing the radiant scenes around us made us feel that it was good to be alive. It was the same jagged ice-field, the same peaks capped with snow, the same monotony of level tundra ; but the shining sun had changed its sombre aspect into one of austere beauty.

The days were dazzlingly bright but at times a thick mist rose from cracks in the sea ice. At regular intervals the ice-field let go with a tremendous roar. After one prolonged, dull reverberation, Akpek remarked :

"Even the ice feels the cold."

Although the sun was above the horizon the temperature still remained at a terribly low level. Throughout January the cold was intense and all wild life disappeared. The foxes, wolves, and rodents stayed buried deep in their holes ; the birds remained hidden in the snow-drifts ; larger game was not to be seen.

No one insufficiently dressed could face the sharp teeth of the bitter cold. I learned that. One day I neglected to cover my head with the hood of my parka.

KABLUK OF THE ESKIMO

I felt an intense pain across my forehead and my sight became blurred. My head spun dizzily and I fell heavily to the ground. Uyarak saw my plight and his prompt action saved me.

Returning to the camp one day, I saw a dog-team before Akpek's igloo. The dogs were lean and they looked weary. The sledge was a strange one, different from those of our party. It was shorter and wider and it had seen hard service.

Upon entering the igloo, I found a man and woman, the latter holding a little baby in her arms. They were the friends Akpek had been waiting for. I looked at them in silence and they stared back.

"Kabluk," said the chief.

The man stepped in front of me. "I am Tupak," he said. "I am not evil. I have no knife."

"I am Kabluk," I answered. "I am friendly."

The woman introduced herself, giving the name of the baby too. We seated ourselves on deerskin pallets and I listened silently while the visitor related his experiences.

"It took us a very long time to get to the land of the musk ox," Tupak said. "After many days spent in crossing the channel and heading into the north, we came to the village of the dwellers-of-the-great-North-land.

"There the travelling was fairly good so long as we followed the tundra along the sea. But, leaving it,

A MESSENGER

we entered hilly country in which the bluffs were tall and the ravines deep, and our way became very rough.

"We came to a region of sandstone and our progress became slow and difficult. I could not keep the mud shoeing under the runners of the sledge for more than a day at a time. At last we could not find mud and we went without the shoeing.

"At the village we found sorrow and gladness. Many of our friends had died; others had moved to other places, following the game they liked best. But there were still many to welcome us.

"A swing of the sun earlier there came a boat to the coast far away to the south and east. It was as long as ten of our kayaks placed end to end, and thick smoke made it move. The men on the boat had heads of fire and hairy faces. Their tempers were quick.

"The strangers landed many bales containing many strange things and they exchanged them for the furry skins of *treganeak*, the fox. It is strange; the traders valued most what we valued least."

"Aha," said Akpek sagely, as Tupak paused to light his pipe.

"Oil and blubber they did not want," our guest continued. "But fox skins they were eager for, especially the silvery ones.

"At first the newcomers were good. But some of them outraged our friends' women. Their chief punished the guilty but our friends would not trade with them any more.

"After they had left, our friends fell ill and many of them died. You sneezed, coughed and became hot all over, shivered as if freezing, went to sleep, died."

"Aha," grunted Akpek. "And the hunt?"

"I stayed at the village until it was time to move on toward the land of the musk ox. On the trail we came across some caribou, but they were small, not at all like those of our land.

"We slept twice twenty times before we reached the hunting country. In all that section there were but three families and it was some time before they would trust us. They were right. They did not know us.

"We stayed on. We became great friends. One day we started out on the hunt for musk ox. We sighted a herd by midday on a flat stretch of tundra land. We approached openly. They saw us coming but they made no effort to get away. The animals only formed a circle with the young in the centre.

"As we neared our quarry, all that we could see was furred backs with long hair hanging down almost to the ground. Their tails moved nervously, but the lumpy shoulders, the horned heads, and the timid eyes of the musk ox were hidden from our sight.

"One of our friends shot an arrow. It struck slanting upwards into the animal's vitals. The victim

A MESSENGER

wedged his head farther into the compact mass, shivered a moment, and fell.

"The animals tightened the circle. One after another they were shot down and the circle grew smaller and smaller until there were no adult beasts left to protect the young. They were dispatched also.

"It was as tame as killing a dog. I have spoken."

Even as we were listening to the tale of Tupak, the other members of the party were preparing for our return to Akpek's village. We returned before the ice went out and I continued on to "The Fort".

CHAPTER XVIII

THE WORLD HAS GONE CRAZY

I RETURNED to the post early in May to find that a daughter had come to my household. My wife was not feeling well; she had worried over my overlong absence. The youngster was as lively as a baby seal, and I got a lot of pleasure playing with her on the floor of the living-room before the roaring blaze.

The trading season was already under way and there was much work to be done. I spent most of the daylight hours in the storehouse, examining furs and checking over my account-books. My evenings were spent in the company of my wife, sitting comfortable, talking or reading.

I was happy, happier than I had ever been before; happier than I have ever been since. My heart was easy; a good wife, a nice baby girl, a cozy home and the friendship of Akpek the chief gave me everything that I desired in life.

In August the *Stord* came again to my little kingdom, bringing a taste of the outer world of civilization. In addition to the regular supplies she carried furniture that I had ordered the previous year for my home. Among

THE WORLD HAS GONE CRAZY

the treasures, which were worth their weight in gold in the isolated spot I had learned to love, was a huge bundle of newspapers and magazines that had appeared during the previous year.

While the boat was with us, I was uncomfortable. There were too many white men around; a gang of roughnecks who did not seem to recognize the grandeur and magnificence of the great country that they traversed in their iron kayak. I was glad when the steamer, our sole link with civilization, vanished in a cloud of smoke on the distant horizon.

The post relapsed into its easygoing stride. The trading season was about over and time hung heavy on my hands through the day, but each evening I spent happily in the company of my family. I smoked my pipe and read my paper with deep enjoyment, even though the news was one year old to the day. Each day I took my paper from the pile, a paper of that exact date—of the previous year.

Through the winter my wife continued to ail; not enough to worry me particularly. Early in the new year the baby was taken down with a bad attack of croup and we worried over her condition.

Remedies suitable for an infant had been left out of the medicine-chest at "The Fort", and I outfitted a small band of Naskopies who wanted to travel into the interior, with the understanding that they were to go on to Rupert House and get the needed medicine. It was a trip of fifteen hundred miles and they did not get back till spring.

Akpek had brought his family to the post. I was glad to see the old patriarch. He had shown me the way to goodness of heart, to peace and contentment. In his company I spent many of the days that followed, sitting quietly and smoking; with him I was never bored, and I never felt the need of trying to make conversation. For hour after hour we would sit communing without uttering a word, but the silence spoke gems of wisdom.

With old Nayume it was a different matter. She called my wife "daughter" and took it upon herself to expound her theories regarding the proper way to bring up infants. It was her expert and capable ministrations that brought the baby back to health.

"My daughter," said old Nayume one day, when the baby was unusually fretful, "when the young of man or animal cries, look to its belly. So my people have taught for more years than you can count."

"Aha, my mother," answered my wife, whom I had taught a smattering of the Eskimo language. "But what must be done?"

"Give the child a piece of seal blubber to suck on," advised Nayume. "It is fine for the bowels."

And so my wife's education in the ways of the Eskimos proceeded. The old woman could never get used to seeing my wife carry the baby around in her

THE WORLD HAS GONE CRAZY

arms; it outraged her sense of the fitness of things to see such a waste of time and energy.

But her constant attention and cheerful kindness to my wife acted as an unfailing tonic, and for the first time since my departure the year previous did I hear my wife's usual hearty laughter. One day old Nayume was helping to bathe the infant in the kitchen, and the baby, helpless in their united grasps, howled with rage. Irritated by the unseemly behaviour, my wife whacked the child's rump a couple of times; and the little one screamed louder than ever.

"Nay, my daughter," expostulated Nayume gently, "the ways of the child are the ways of the father; and you must handle your daughter as you handle your man. You must be patient."

"Aha, my mother," said my wife, half ashamed of her ill-temper. "That is so; but the child——"

"Is wiser than the man," said Nayume, interrupting. "It cries only when there is reason to cry."

Akpek removed his pipe from his mouth and smiled soberly.

"Women talk like ptarmigan," he said, "Ka, ka, ka."

Early in the spring, word came to the post that an Eskimo family belonging to the Takamio tribe, while hunting seals at the edge of the sea, had been trapped by a sudden shift of the ice. Caught by the strong swift current they had been swept far from land, and all of their kayaks had been lost but one. In a desperate attempt to reach the rapidly receding shore-line, one of the hunters had taken to the kayak, but, caught in the swirl of the onrushing water, he was thrown upon the bleak, rocky coast. There searchers had found him, still fastened to the kayak.

The terrible news reminded the chief that he had long overstayed his accustomed time at the post. My wife tried to get them to stay for a few weeks longer; but Akpek pointed out that it was near the time when the tribe was due to remove to their summer camp on the island, and I made no effort to detain him.

Summer came. Trapping had been good and trading was above the average. The ice was late in going out in 1915, and it was not until the middle of August that a plume of smoke in the northern sky announced the coming of the annual steamer.

It was the same old *Stord*, but this time she had a new captain, a grizzled and weatherworn old veteran of many whaling cruises in the Arctic. I took him up to my place to get acquainted. I motioned him to a seat and, getting a bottle of Canadian Club whisky, I placed it upon the table between us. It was the only invitation he needed and he poured himself a stiff hooker. He waited until I had poured myself a drink.

"Here's how," he boomed in a deep-sea voice.

The captain downed his drink neat, without the

THE WORLD HAS GONE CRAZY

bat of an eye. I drank mine more slowly, savouring the taste of the liquor as it trickled down my gullet.

"Well," said the captain, rubbing his lips with the back of his hand, "we've pushed them back from Paris."

"What?" I queried, looking at him in surprise.

"The Boche," he explained. "We've chased them from the gates of Paris."

"I don't understand you," I said. "What is it—this Boche?"

"Boche, Boche," growled the captain, thinking I was making fun of him. "The Germans."

"*Diable!*" I retorted. "What about them?"

"Say," said the captain, looking at me queerly, "don't you know that the Germans nearly took Paris?"

"Come, Captain," I answered, getting angry. "I do not like this foolishness. What are you getting at?"

"The war. . . ."

"War?" I repeated uncomprehendingly. "What war?"

"The war of the nations," he explained. "All of the countries of Europe are at war. Even Canada is sending an army to France."

"*Mon Dieu!*" I cried.

The captain rose to go but I detained him. "Tell me," I asked, "just what has happened. There was no news of a war when the steamer came last year."

"I thought you knew," my companion answered. "It is too long to explain, though. Come on down to the boat and I will give you the latest newspapers. You will get the whole story from them."

As we walked to the shore he gave me fragmentary snatches of the main events that had taken place since the arrival of the previous steamer.

France at war! That was serious news. I held the rank of Lieutenant of Reserves in the French Army and was subject to mobilization orders. I had heard nothing as yet but the call might come at any time. Perhaps it might be among the letters brought by the boat, I thought; but a careful check did not bring it to light.

The next few days I spent in skimming through the batch of newspapers he had given me.

"*Mon Dieu!*" I said to my wife. "The whole world has gone crazy."

One thing occupied my mind to the exclusion of all else. Although I had not been called as yet to the colours, as a soldier it was my duty to return to France. My mind was made up and I wrote to headquarters in Montreal, asking that I be relieved when the steamer returned to Ungava the following year.

When the *Stord* turned her nose seaward, the letter was aboard; and with it went my peace of mind. I stood upon the river's bank, and watched the vessel until it vanished around a turn in the channel, and my mind was filled with vague forebodings.

I had a great longing to go and visit the chief, and

THE WORLD HAS GONE CRAZY

as soon as things quieted down at the post I went. Ten years had gone by since I had first met Akpek: ten years of learning to live, to be contented and happy. And now . . . everything was becoming unreal, as though an evil spell had me in its grip.

It was late in the winter when I reached the village on the main shore. The igloos gleamed in the light of the hidden sun and it was evident that the ice would be going out early.

Akpek greeted me with his kindly smile. In the tent Nayume fixed me a bite to eat; she was concerned that I did not eat with my usual gusto, but I had little appetite for the special dishes she had prepared to celebrate my coming.

"My son," said Akpek gravely, after I had finished eating, "you do not look well."

I puffed at my pipe in silence, staring at the ground in a moody abstraction. "My father," I said at last, "I have come to say farewell."

Akpek pondered my remark for an hour or more in silence. "You will return?" he queried finally.

"I do not know."

"That is strange." The chief inhaled deeply; I remained silent, and after a long pause he queried:

"Why do you leave us?"

"I must return to my own country."

Akpek was puzzled. "What does that funny word—'country'—mean?"

"It is a word for tribe in the land from where I came."

Again the chief was silent, meditating upon my unusual words. It was a quietness that suited me.

"Where does your tribe live?" he asked.

"Far beyond the great sea, my father."

"How far?"

I thought long for a way to make myself clear. "The distance is very great," I said. "Suppose you travelled by dog-team for as many sleeps as there are in two dips of the sun—then you will only be reaching the edge of my homeland."

"Aha," grunted Akpek, shaking his grey head. "It is indeed far away."

While we sat conversing, a hullabaloo outside came faintly to our ears through the snow walls. It was the return of a party of seal hunters who had bagged a full dozen of the mammals. Anotinoak, the tusked one, thrust himself through the opening of the igloo and informed us of the kill.

"There will be many bellies filled with seal meat to-night," he said with a grin.

We went outside. The hunters were busily at work cutting up the carcasses at the edge of the ice, while a circle of women and children stood admiringly looking on and chattering. The dogs squatted with hanging tongues, giving vent to short sharp yelps.

The days passed. The sun peeped above the

THE WORLD HAS GONE CRAZY

horizon for a brief instant one day and the weather turned very warm. That night the ice went out. In the morning we found that a rippling expanse of water separated us from the island.

"It will soon be time for my people to move to the summer camp," said Akpek, as he stood on the shore and gazed across the channel, and he sighed deeply.

I said nothing and he went on:

"It will not be the same without Kabluk." As I still did not answer, he turned and walked slowly back to his igloo. Inside we found Nayume disrobing Amaluke, preparatory to clothing her in a new *shelepak*. She smiled kindly but said nothing, and the little girl laughed as her mother's fingers tickled her bare skin.

Akpek seated himself in his accustomed place but I stood leaning against the icy wall. We smoked, and I watched the smoke eddy and swirl upward as the chief emitted vast exhalations of breath.

"My son," said Akpek, "I have thought long of your departure."

"Aha, my father."

"Are you not well looked after?" he queried. "Do not my people bring plenty of furs to your habitation?"

"It is not that," I answered slowly.

The cold wall sent a chill through my shoulder and I seated myself upon a pile of soft caribou mats. It was stuffy in the igloo and Nayume went outside to erect the tent, with her little daughter following at her heels.

"Why must you go back to your tribe?" asked Akpek after a prolonged silence.

"I go to fight for my tribe," I said. "An enemy is invading my tribe's land."

"That is bad, my son," grunted the chief gravely. "Why does another tribe bother your people?"

"I do not know, my father," I answered with a shake of my head, adding, "I do not think that they know themselves."

"Very strange," mumbled Akpek, lost in thought, his mind seeking a solution to the problem. "It is very strange."

I knocked the ashes from the bowl of my pipe and refilled it slowly, meditatively. The seamed face of the chief was immobile except for regular, deep movement of his lips as he sucked upon his pipe.

"You must go," he said, looking at me with a sad smile. "*Ayunamat!*—it cannot be helped."

"It is the way of my people," I assented. "We must answer the call of the big chief; we must fight to protect our women, our homes, our property."

"Aha! You must do that."

Nayume entered, bringing a stone kettle of steaming caribou-blood soup. Her face was sweaty and she wiped it on the sleeve of her costume. She put the pot down between us and we began to eat.

THE WORLD HAS GONE CRAZY

"The tent is ready," she said to her husband, "by the willows."

"Good," snorted Akpek, between great gulps of the hot soup. "We will sleep there to-night."

During the night the wind blew from the north and the channel that separated us from the island was filled with broken ice. As the days passed the channel again rippled clear and free.

Down at the shore men and women were busy preparing for the annual move to their island encampment. The umiaks, piled high with equipment, made trip after trip, until all of the paraphernalia had been ferried across. And before the sun reached its topmost point the village was ready for occupancy.

With Akpek I walked up and down the shore. "You will go when the 'iron kayak' comes for the furs?" he inquired.

"Aha, my father."

"Your tribe must be great," he said after a pause.

"Why?"

"To fight for so long."

"It is so," I answered. "In my country the war is very great; big. Many tribes are fighting."

Taking a stick, I drew a wavering line and on either side lined many smaller ones. Pointing to the latter, I explained:

"Many, many tribes are fighting each other. Those on each side of the line are friends."

KABLUK OF THE ESKIMO

"Ha," grunted Akpek knowingly and, taking the stick from my hand, he drew a line that cut through the smaller ones, saying, "Here is many tribes of Eskimo. They are friendly."

"That is so, my father."

"Here are many herds of *ai'vuk*," he went on, cutting a gash on the other side of the main line with a swift stroke. "They are friends.

"Each band to fight the other."

"That is right," I said, pleased at his perception. "It is a big battle. Each day many, many men are killed."

"As many as the caribou we kill each season?"

"Many, many, many more," I answered. "There are so many men killed each day that if they were laid side by side it would take two sleeps by dog-team to reach the end of the line."

"Is it possible?" asked the chief, amazed. "Your people must be as numerous as the flies in summer."

"Aha, my father," I said. "There is no word in your language to describe the number. Take each dog in the Eskimo country and multiply them by twenty times twenty: there will not be enough to equal the number of my people."

Three times we walked up the shore and three times back before Akpek spoke again. Taking his pipe from his mouth, he asked:

"Where does your people get enough blubber to

THE WORLD HAS GONE CRAZY

feed on, enough hide and furs to clothe and shoe themselves? Is it possible that *ai'vuk* is more plentiful elsewhere? And the other animals too?"

"No, my father," I said. "In my country we live on white man's food; food that grows in the ground like the berries that abound in your land."

"You eat no blubber? No flesh?"

"Our meat," I answered, "is like that of the caribou."

Akpek shook his head. "Your land is not for me or mine," he grunted. "Without blubber we would die."

During the days that followed I spent most of my time communing with the chief. One day, when I was feeling cranky, I borrowed a kayak and paddled across to the main shore. I wanted to be alone, away from all men.

I travelled leisurely along the coast. At night and during the intervals of low tide I put in to shore and camped. Every foot of the way brought back recollections of happy hours. I came to the place of the caribou hunt. The slightly rolling meadowland was covered with purple flowers; the grass was tall and green; in a section of swampy land, low bushes teemed with growing berries; and over all there hung a wild sweet fragrance.

Leaving the kayak upon the shore I walked inland. All over, half covered by the vegetation, were bleaching bones of butchered caribou, picked clean by

KABLUK OF THE ESKIMO

amorok, the wolf, the scavenger of the Arctic. The skeletons made me think of dead men, slain men, war.

I turned back to the village. It was late in the afternoon of the third day when I doubled the spit of land that hid the habitations. The chief was pacing slowly to and fro, as was his usual custom.

That night, after eating, I told him that I was going to return to the post. He looked me straight in the eyes for several minutes.

"You must go," he said, adding, "I would not have you stay."

We talked and the hours flew by. Nayume and Amaluke, the little girl, went to sleep, but still we talked. We spoke of many things, but chiefly of war.

"How do your people fight?" queried the chief. "On water or on land?"

"Both, my father," I answered. "And under the surface and above the surface too."

"How can that be?"

"We have iron boats like the whale, but many times bigger," I explained. "It comes to the top of the water for air like *ai'vuk*; and it shoots great iron darts at enemy ships."

"Ah!" marvelled the chief.

"Through the air," I went on, "we send kayaks with wings. A big paddle that whirls around and around sends it through the air and a man guides it."

THE WORLD HAS GONE CRAZY

"Ah! Ah!" grunted Akpek again. "They must be bad birds."

"Aha," I answered.

Akpek smoked in silence. Through the opening of the tent I saw the faint flush of the coming dawn against a background of broken clouds. A murmuring breeze swept through the ridgepoles of the tents and I heard the sweep of the surf upon the distant shore.

"Do your men fight with harpoons?" said the chief, breaking the long silence. "Or do they use lances?"

"Our weapons, my father," I answered, "are strange and fearful. We have guns as big as a tree that shoot bullets as big as a fox and the bullets explode like thunder.

"Over the battlefield rumble huge monsters. They look like umiaks turned upside down and sheathed with iron; they go everywhere and nothing can stop them.

"That is how my people fight."

"That is not the way of the Eskimos," commented Akpek. "It is bad—very bad."

"Aha, my father," I answered. "You are right."

The climbing sun sent its rays along the island's ridge. It was daylight. Together we went outside and walked to the shore. In silence we paced back and forth until Nayume called us to breakfast.

After I had eaten, I went down to the place where the kayaks rested. As I prepared for my departure, the rest of the villagers came down to see me off. Akpek and Nayume stood stolidly at the side of the main group and I walked over to them.

"I am ready to go, my father," I said. "Will you come to the post before the *Stord* comes?"

"Aha, my son," Akpek answered gravely.

"And you, my mother?"

"I too, my son," she said, with a full heart.

I turned away and strode to the water's edge. Taking my place in the kayak, I pushed off from the shore, and, raising my paddle over my head, I shouted:

"*Chimo!*"

A full-throated roar came from the assemblage.

"*Chimo!*" they shouted.

Bending to my work, I sent my kayak skimming toward the mainland. The current swept me on my way and the shore receded rapidly. A quick glance over my shoulder showed me the figure of the chief standing alone with bent head, and then a scarp of rock hid him from view.

At the post, trading went on as usual; I had my account-books to balance and I instructed Berthe so that he would be able to take my place.

Late in July the *Stord* came up the Koksoak. She was early and Akpek had not yet arrived. With a heavy heart I saw her tie up to the ramshackle pier at the riverside. I went aboard and sought out the captain. From him I received my orders, relieving

THE WORLD HAS GONE CRAZY

me from further duty at the post and appointing Berthe in my place.

Late on the second day after the arrival of the steamer, shouts from the no-account "White Men" and Indians sent me outside to see what the uproar was about. They were staring down-river.

An armada of kayaks was coming up the river. It was Akpek and his people. One by one the watercraft drew in to shore and the occupants debarked. I ran down to greet them.

"*Chimo!*" I shouted, waving my hand.

"*Chimo!*" answered my friends in a rapid crackle of many voices. "Kabluk; *Chimo!*"

While his people set about making camp, I took Akpek to the house. I gave him my tobacco-jar and bade him fill his pipe. My wife appeared, coming down the stairway.

"*Chimo*, my father," she said. "You are doubly welcome at this time."

"Partings are sad, my daughter," answered Akpek

"Aha," she agreed, and, turning to me, she said, "I will see to Nayume."

"The old woman is by the camp site," the chief informed her. My wife went to fetch Nayume.

We smoked in silence for a while. "The boat leaves to-morrow," I announced.

"Ha!" grunted Akpek; he said nothing further until after we had eaten. Then, as he was leaving to go to his tent, he remarked, "Akpek and his people will never forget Kabluk."

"But I will return, my father. When the war is over—I feel it—I will return—if I am alive."

"Aha," sighed the old chief, "my son Kabluk will return."

In the morning I boarded the *Stord* with my family. I said my farewells to Berthe and his men on deck; they trooped ashore; the gangplank was drawn aboard; and with the mournful wailing of our siren, we cast off and dropped slowly down the stream. As we did so, the kayaks of Akpek the chief took to the water and fell into line behind us.

Akpek led the van, his paddle flashing bravely in the sun as he swung it with a steady, rhythmical stroke, and behind him paddled the kayaks of his people.

The engine of the *Stord* laboured, throbbing, and the propeller sent a swirl of water behind her. As she gained speed, we left the armada farther and farther to the rear. The kayaks danced on the rough water left by the churning propeller. I saw the chief cease paddling.

Akpek stood upright for a moment and raised his paddle high above his head in a gesture of farewell. I waved in answer. A sharp turn in the channel cut him from my sight and I went below.

I was leaving happiness behind me, but I felt that in time I would return and reconquer that happiness.

CHAPTER XIX

FROM ICE TO FIRE

THE *Stord* wallowed around the northern tip of the Labrador and turned her nose southward bound for Newfoundland. Our first contact with civilization came when we touched at St. John's and I took the family ashore to see the sights of the town.

"Oh!" cried the youngster, pointing in round-eyed surprise at a horse. "Look at the big dog."

It was the first domesticated animal she had ever seen, outside of the omnipresent dogs at "The Fort". To her everything was new and strange.

Immediately upon landing at our destination, I placed my family in lodgings and reported at the company offices. I was expecting mobilization orders from my Government, but they had not come yet and, having settled my affairs with my employers, I decided that there was time to escort my family to Moose Factory, where my wife's folks still lived.

It was a long journey, and I did not get back to Montreal until late the following spring. Still there was no word from the Army authorities. Mystified, I went to the French Consul and explained matters, and he sent me to New York with orders to sail for France on the steamship *Rochambeau*.

I was in New York, that vast beehive of humanity, for only a day or so, but it was long enough to demonstrate that life in the Arctic was infinitely preferable to the maddening conditions of the civilized world, and I thought with longing of Akpek and his people and their quiet simplicity.

The *Rochambeau* carried a number of reservists, and we had a fine time together most of the way across the Atlantic. Near the edge of the submarine zone we were joined by a number of other vessels also bound for Bordeaux. We were taken in hand by a squadron of destroyers and with every light doused we sailed into the danger zone.

There were twenty-seven ships in our convoy, and the *Rochambeau*, the biggest of the lot, was in the centre. We were not far from our destination when a wireless message announced that there were submarines in our vicinity. The hours passed without any untoward incidents and by lunchtime most of us had forgotten about the matter. Suddenly a dull boom brought us to our feet. In an instant all thought of food was forgotten and we rushed for the deck. I got there just in time to see the ship that followed us in the convoy lift her stern high into the air and plunge. It was a terrible sight and it recalled to my mind the final dive of a mortally wounded walrus.

FROM ICE TO FIRE

The other boats in the convoy at the first sign of trouble had scattered to the four winds, and the *Rochambeau* was zigzagging erratically; travelling at a tremendous pace, the destroyers searched the debris-strewn water for the submarine and at intervals the rapid bark of quick-firers sounded.

"Holloa!" shouted someone on the bridge. At the same moment I saw a streak of white heading for us amidship. The *Rochambeau* was on a tack and the wheelsman threw the vessel farther over; slowly, God knows how slowly, the ship swung out of the path of the onrushing torpedo.

From where I stood, up forward, it seemed that we were clear, but the sound of a loud explosion indicated otherwise. The *Rochambeau* heaved slightly at the stern. The torpedo had struck the rudder and exploded, tearing away a large section; but otherwise the ship was undamaged and we continued our course until we were safely away.

A dozen miles or so from Bordeaux we passed a ship that was afire. She was loaded with a cargo of cotton and the submarine that ended her career had sent two torpedoes into her without sinking her, but they had set her afire. The undersea boat that did the dirty work was not to be seen when we passed. We steamed into the harbour and on up the river to Bordeaux without further trouble.

As soon as the debarking formalities were over I

went to military headquarters and reported for duty. A colonel checked a list for my name. He looked up.

"Why are you so late," he queried.

"I did not know that France was at war," I answered.

"What?" he barked. "You do not expect me to believe that."

"I do," I retorted. "I did not know that there was a war."

"You will find out that this is not a time to joke, *mon ami*," the colonel growled. "You have evaded your duty."

"I have not."

"Then why are you so late in reporting for duty?"

"I have just come from a part of the world," I explained, "where news of the war has hardly penetrated even now. In the Arctic, events a year old are still news, and when I heard of the war I immediately wrote out, asking to be relieved from my post."

"Even so," said the colonel, "the war is nearly three years old. You should have reported before this."

"When I got to civilization," I returned, "I waited for the mobilization order, but it did not come. And at last I went to our Consul and reported to him. He arranged for my passage to France and here I am."

The officer heard me out without interrupting me further and when I had finished he said:

"You have papers to prove your statements?"

"In my luggage."

FROM ICE TO FIRE

"That is fine," said the colonel; he paused and scanned the records of my service again. "You were a Lieutenant of the Reserve?"

"*Oui, mon colonel.*"

"Your commission has been cancelled," said the officer, staring at me; "the war has done many things that none of us anticipated."

I remained silent and he continued:

"It is necessary that you learn the ways of modern warfare. I will send you to the training-camp at Pau as a sergeant, and you can make up for lost time there."

He indicated that the interview was over and I went outside to reflect. Little time was given to me and by nightfall I was speeding across the terrain of La Belle France en route to the training-camp.

At Pau, I went through the ordeal by question again and at its conclusion the Commandant said:

"Well, *mon ami*, I will see that you make up for the time that you have lost among the Eskimos. You will be trained in short order."

I did not like the life at the training-camp; there was too much noise and hurry. But I did not stay there long. In twelve days I was on my way to the front, to Verdun.

Always it was rush, rush, rush—by train, by truck, by forced marches. And the noise! It increased as we went forward. I never did get used to the cannonading, and when I heard the crump of high explosive it reminded me of a huge mass of ice crashing from a frozen cliff.

Then came the horrible life in the trenches—the noise, the terror, the blood, the filth. The ways of the Eskimos were not what most people would consider neat, tidy or elegant; ah, but their ways seemed like a sublime height of all that is clean and pure beside the mud, the slime and the lice of the trenches.

I was in at the taking of Fort Douamont. For hours our artillery—*Mon Dieu!* how those seventy-fives pounded away—swept the enemy trenches with an unrelenting fire, and I wondered how any living creature could exist in that man-made inferno.

All night we waited. Some slept, some could not sleep. We went over the top just before sunrise, a line of men plodding across the blasted earth, while the artillery thundered. For a while the going was easy. Then the Germans crawled from their holes, cutting loose at us with machine-guns. Men dropped on all sides, but it was too late to stop us, and we were in amongst them with cold steel.

I encountered a big, good-natured looking Boche; he was grinning for some reason and as he jabbed at me with his bayonet, he grunted heavily. For me, using a bayonet was like using an Eskimo harpoon. I sidestepped his thrust, and before my assailant could jump back I let him have my bayonet right through his belly.

FROM ICE TO FIRE

The German sagged to his knees, dragging me down; with a violent wrench I yanked my bayonet out of his carcass, spilling his guts over the ground. A heavy gush of his blood caught me right in the face. It sickened me, and, as I swabbed the sticky mess off, so that I could see, I remembered the caribou hunt I had been on with Akpek and his tribe.

We arrived at our objective and dug in. There were a number of counter-attacks and gradually things died down.

In the trenches we resumed the regular routine of warfare in a quiet sector. At intervals we were relieved and sent to the rear, but our stays in the billets were all too short for me.

It was always the interminable time of the trenches—day after day in discomfort and hardship and in the presence of death. I thought of the long days in the Arctic, the off-season at the post, or the winter at Akpek's village, immured in igloos while the blizzard raged; but that seemed a time of entertainment and the swift passage of happy hours beside the dull heaviness of life in the trenches.

Now and then there would come a little flare-up in our sector, a bit of fighting to keep our hands in. The artillery would lay its barrage and we would go over the top. When we didn't want to play, the enemy did, so there was usually something to keep us awake.

We were lined up in the trench one morning for

one of those little parties. The seventy-fives were pounding away in great style and the enemy artillery was trying to return the compliment, but without much success. The zero hour was set for eight o'clock.

I stood beside the senior sergeant of my company, a fellow named Duthil. He was a tall, thin fellow; as brave as they come and as phlegmatic as an Englishman. There was still a few minutes of grace before the fun started, and I was making the best of it with a canteen of the famous Pinar wine. I said:

"Have a drink, *mon ami*?"

"No," he answered soberly. "No, thanks."

"No?" I was surprised, and I showed it.

"I don't feel like drinking right now," he explained.

I stared at him. "What's the matter, Duthil?" I asked. "You look blue."

He said nothing. His eye was glued to the face of his watch. He was counting the seconds as they ticked away into eternity. I took another swig from the canteen.

"Two more minutes," said Duthil irrelevantly, and, turning to me, he went on, "Here is my watch; would you mind keeping it for me?"

"What for?" I asked, looking at him curiously.

"Oh," he answered negligently. "You never can tell what will happen out there."

"Surely you don't think——" I began.

FROM ICE TO FIRE

"*Non, non, mon ami,*" he interrupted, squirming under my questioning gaze.

What can you do with a man like that? He was certain that he was going to his death in a few minutes. I took the watch.

We went over the top, expecting that we would surprise the enemy, but they turned the tables on us. Their zero hour was a few seconds before ours, and when we clambered out of the trench, the Boche was already coming at us. We came together out in the middle of No Man's Land. Holloa! What a mess!

I had a revolver in my hand and Duthil was beside me, carrying a rifle. In the mêlée it was hard to distinguish things clearly; the ground was covered with a slight haze. A huge German loomed up, and before I could make a move to prevent him, he jabbed me in the belly with his bayonet; Duthil saw my predicament and with a lightning-like thrust he knocked the enemy's gun upward, and the bayonet came out, leaving a long cut in my hide. The wound was about two inches deep and it was bad enough to put me out of the scrap.

I was in agony and bleeding like a harpooned walrus. Through a deepening haze I saw Duthil feint and let the big Boche have the cold steel right through his chest; as he drew back to loosen his bayonet a form loomed behind him. A German lurched with a terrible thrust of his bayonet and nailed my comrade to the ground. I fainted.

KABLUK OF THE ESKIMO

When I woke up I was in an ambulance, on my way to the rear; my wound had been attended to and I did not suffer much. But I was in for a stretch of hospital life. The days dragged. Mutilated men were brought in, hundreds, hundreds. They died, they lingered, they got well. In a few weeks I was up and about, a *blessé*; and when the gash in my midriff had healed up, I was ordered to the air service for duty as an observer. And now it was the terror of the sky.

I was assigned to do artillery spotting. I sat in a cubbyhole. Behind me was the pilot and we communicated with each other over a kind of telephone.

An enemy battery was doing a lot of damage in our territory. It was well camouflaged and the squadron had a difficult time trying to find it. I had an idea of its location and I decided to end its career of destruction. I had my pilot circle the place at a fair altitude.

"Dive!" I called to the pilot.

Down, down, down we went. From my position in the front cockpit I saw the ground coming at me with a dizzy rush, and, peeping through a cover of green boughs, I caught the glint of the barrel of a fieldpiece. Anti-aircraft guns were popping away at us.

The pilot held the plane's nose down, and just as I felt that we would never come out of the dive, he pulled back on the stick. The plane zoomed up and away from the hail of steel that was flying all around us. At that moment an anti-aircraft shell burst just above us,

FROM ICE TO FIRE

right in my face, it seemed. The fragments cut through the wings of the machine.

The flying pieces cut my face to ribbons. I could not see anything and my face was covered with blood.

"Turn back!" I shouted.

We got back without further trouble, although the enemy anti-aircraft guns were concentrating their fire upon us. I was taken to the hospital immediately. My face looked like a lump of seal blubber, but my eyes were all right. As soon as I was fit to travel I was sent to a hospital in the south of France, to have my features restored.

The place had formerly been a college. In the ward I was in there were one hundred and twenty-five patients of all nationalities—French, English, American, Italian, Chinese and French colonials—and to attend to us there was only one nurse.

That poor woman I venerate more than my own mother. Day and night she was on call, and I have seen her so exhausted that she would throw herself on a bed, from which the dead had just been removed, and cat-nap until the monotonous call of "Nurse, nurse", would ring through the vast room.

I was taken down with the flu and for a time it seemed as if I were going to die. Pneumonia had set in and for days on end I was delirious. In one of my lucid moments I heard the doctor speaking to the nurse.

"Ninety-nine will be gone by midnight," he said, as he stood at my bedside. And I was ninety-nine.

"Too bad," said the angel, soothing my brow with her soft touch. She sighed and went about her multitude of duties. So, I thought, I am going to die; well, *ayunamat*, it cannot be helped. And I recalled Akpek to mind momentarily, hazily. Again delirium gripped me and I slowly slid toward the brink of the grave.

Suddenly I seemed to wake with a start and found myself lying beside a deserted road. I got up and stared down the dark thoroughfare; on my right hand the avenue was lined with trees without leaves, bare; on the left was a high wall and its end was hidden in the dusk. Above, the sky was covered with clouds which hung without motion, yet the trees bent as though under the lash of a storm.

I travelled along the road and it was getting darker and darker all of the time. At last I neared the end of the road and in vague outline I saw a poorhouse; in front of it I saw a shadowy figure, and as I came nearer I saw that it was a woman.

I paused. There was no wind, and yet her hair was flowing and whipping about and her dress flapped violently. Resuming my way, I saw that she had her hands extended behind her in a protecting way and I sensed that she was shielding her children. With a start I stopped dead in my tracks; the woman was my wife and she was sheltering our children.

FROM ICE TO FIRE

My wife was thin, dressed in rags; and the children looked as though they were starved. It was a most pitiful sight and my heart contracted at the evident suffering of my loved ones. My wife a pauper, I thought with horror. Impossible! I cannot die.

At the thought, the tightness left my heart; everything seemed to brighten and yet to fade away. I stood alone, and then the world darkened, and I was awake once more.

When the doctor made his rounds in the morning, I was sitting up in bed. "What time did ninety-nine go?" he asked the nurse casually, without looking at me.

"That is ninety-nine," said the nurse, nodding toward me.

From that time on I was a nine-days' wonder among the doctors and nurses in the hospital. From the nurse in my ward I got the details of what had happened during the night. Shortly after midnight she had come to my bedside; she felt my pulse; there was none. I was dead. She called a couple of stretcher-bearers to take me out, and with her own hands closed my eyes. The orderlies lifted me off the bed and dropped me on to the stretcher.

The fall of my body must have coincided with the feeling of relief in my dream, and the combined stimulus sent a life-giving rush of blood through my veins. I groaned and woke up, to the surprise of everybody.

I was still a very sick man, and my nurse, with her special care, really saved my life in the five months of severe illness that followed. My siege of sickness made an old man of me. For the first time I felt my age. I got better in body; in mind I became moody and irritable. I longed for the vast, illimitable spaces of the north country with an intense longing. Akpek and his people filled my thoughts.

The war came to an end, but my condition was such that it was impossible for me to return home. I ate my heart out in vain, hoping that my turn would soon come, and my hatred of civilization grew. I longed to get away to the North.

I was finally demobilized. I went to London and after a short visit took ship for home in July 1919. I was still sick at heart, weak, a changed man; but when I saw the bleak shores of Canada, my heart overflowed with happiness.

Upon my arrival at Montreal I had sent for my family. From Moose Factory they came to Cochrane by canoe, where I met them. My meeting with my wife was very simple, as is the way of the North, but we were very happy to be together again.

In the months that followed, my physical health became better, but my mental state grew steadily worse. Life in Montreal, with its noise and its meaningless activities, grew unbearable. The grave face of Akpek beckoned with promise of peace and quietude, and with

FROM ICE TO FIRE

the coming of winter I turned my face toward the Arctic country.

I went overland, made a long journey by sledge to Ungava. It was a painful and disagreeable trip. My old adventurous spirit, my old physical buoyancy were gone. The war had sapped my strength and I was not equal to those hard Arctic journeys that I had formerly made so joyfully.

At "The Fort" things were about the same—but they were different to me. The furs, the trading, the Indians, the worthless Eskimo "White Men" disgusted me. Everything was a great disappointment to me. A veil had fallen from my eyes and for the first time I was seeing the harsh bleakness of the North.

I did not stop long at "The Fort". It held no lure for me, and I went directly to Akpek's village on the fringe of the frozen sea.

CHAPTER XX

MY FATHER, I HAVE CHANGED

IT was late in the afternoon when I came into sight of Akpek's village, sprawling at the edge of the frozen sea. Clouds blanketed the sky and the rounded domes of the igloos dully reflected the faint light that filtered through from above.

I pulled up my dog-team and stood staring at the familiar scene that lay spread out before me. The villagers were at their evening meal; but for the wreaths of smoke ascending into the still air, there was nothing to show that human life existed so close at hand. Not a sound broke the uncanny stillness. I stood in a dead world, a vast immensity of nothingness.

As I gazed, an overwhelming sense of the futility of human existence gripped me and I was overcome with an intolerable sorrow. I had changed beyond recall, I brooded. Nothing could ever bring back to me the happiness I had once known, æons ago. My peace of mind had irretrievably vanished into the horrible maelstrom of war, of civilization.

A movement in the village caught my eye. A dog had emerged from the entrance to an igloo and it squatted

I HAVE CHANGED

on its haunches, with lolling tongue and slavering jaws. The other dogs in the village followed at intervals and soon the whole pack was waiting in expectant silence. The evening meal was over and the dogs were about to be fed.

I called to my team. The sledge started with a jerk and at a rapid gait we swept down the slight declivity that terminated at the edge of the ice-bound sea. The yapping and howling of the dogs in the village announced my arrival and the igloos spewed forth their occupants.

In the crowd of smiling Eskimos that surrounded me I saw many familiar faces. Some I knew very well, others were vaguely familiar, and a few were entire strangers. But they were one in their smiles of welcome.

"Kabluk," grunted Uyarak, stepping forward. "*Chimo.*"

"*Chimo,*" I answered and began to unharness my team. The men were silent, staring in polite curiosity; the women chattered unceasingly, bandying smart remarks and laughing immoderately. Among them, noisiest of all, was Norrak, wearing the costume of the married woman. When I glanced at her she stared at me brazenly, and I felt sorry for the man who had taken her for wife.

I finished untangling the traces and stood up.

"The igloo of Akpek will be happy this day," wheezed a hoary-headed elder, as I followed Uyarak to the chief's habitation; the villagers answered with a chorus of "Aha" and the crowd melted away.

Inside the igloo I found the chief. "*Chimo*, my son," quavered old Akpek, as he rose to his feet.

"*Chimo*, my father," I answered, staring intently at the dim figure that sat motionless upon the ice shelf.

Gradually my eyes became accustomed to the gloom. The skin mats were scattered as usual, in a corner the old stone lamp smoked, on the other side of the chamber the chief's favourite harpoon leaned against the ice wall, damp clothes were drying on the line; the igloo was much the same as of yore; yet I sensed an indefinable difference.

I placed myself upon a pallet of caribou skins and filled my pipe. We smoked in silence. Nayume came in, bearing a pot of blood soup which she placed beside me. I did not want to hurt the old woman's feelings and I forced myself to eat some of it, although my gorge rose and I almost choked on the vile mixture.

"Do not eat, my son," said Akpek gravely. "Your stomach is not hungry for food."

"That is so, my father," I responded, and, putting the pot to one side, I resumed my reclining position on the pallet. Nayume was at work on the raw hide of a baby seal, and the fetid stink of the hide irritated my nostrils. I puffed heavily on my pipe to eliminate it, and through the haze I stared at the calm nobility of Akpek's face. By imperceptible degrees the serene

I HAVE CHANGED

majesty of his careworn features made me forget the petty irritations that irked me.

While I was lost in contemplation there was a noise at the entrance and Uyarak came in. He squatted against the wall but said nothing. His arrival was soon followed by the other men of the village; old men with whom I had travelled and hunted, young men who had been youngsters when I had left to go among the evil influences of the civilized world. Most took their places in silence, smiling in welcome; a few greeted me with a brief word.

"My son," grunted the aged chief tremulously. "You have travelled far."

"Aha, yes," I said. "I have travelled far and seen much."

And I went on to describe the events of my journey to civilization and return as briefly as possible. My audience listened in silence for the most part, giving grunts of approval at infrequent intervals.

"From far to the south I came by *komutik*," I said finally. "I am here. I have spoken."

"My son," grunted the chief, "Akpek and his people have missed you."

There came a succession of vibrant assents from the others in the igloo and I felt impelled to answer.

"Aha," I said slowly, "and the heart of Kabluk has been empty."

Thus, in the conventional phrases of their own

tongue, I responded to the attempts of my friends to welcome me back into their midst, but it was with a heavy heart. I knew only too well that "Kabluk of the Eskimo" existed no longer; he had vanished in the mad dissolution of destructive war.

The chief puffed sedately on his stone pipe and for a time all was silent. I glanced around the chamber, seeking a glimpse of an old friend.

"I do not see Anotinoak, the tusked one," I said finally.

"He is not here," answered Uyarak and he mumbled an incantation under his breath.

I failed to grasp his meaning and I asked:

"When will he return?"

A pregnant silence fell upon the group and no one answered. I began to surmise the answer but I turned to Akpek for confirmation.

"Anotinoak, the tusked one," the chief said in measured tones, "has gone to the regions below. Evil spirits entered his body at the time when the caribou have calves. He died."

While the chief was speaking, a few of the younger men slipped away, for death is a subject with many taboos and their superstitious souls were afraid of the possible return of the spirit of the old craftsman.

Old Nayume, who had been visiting friends in order to be out of the way until the ceremonies attendant upon my return had been concluded, came in with Amaluke

I HAVE CHANGED

and they went to bed, but I sat with the chief in silent communion.

"The night is far gone," said Akpek finally. "I am weary. I will sleep."

He stretched himself out and in a short time was snoring heavily. For some time I lay awake, thinking, thinking bitterly. Why had I returned to this wilderness of ice and snow? I asked myself questions which I could not answer, until finally sleep came.

In the morning I joined my friends in their pastimes but I found that their simple games and tricks no longer had the power to amuse me. Something had gone out of my life and now a harpoon was just a harpoon to me, a *komutik* another sledge, and an Eskimo a primitive member of the human species.

Under the beneficent influence of Akpek, however, I spent much of the time sitting staring at the stern nobility of his corrugated features. So the days passed slowly. Under the tender ministrations of old Nayume I slowly regained something of my former strength, but it was impossible for me to find the permanent peace of mind which I had lost. The chief sensed my moodiness and one day he said:

"My son, you are not the same."

"No, my father," I answered, staring at the ground. "I have changed."

"*Ayunamat*—my son," grunted Akpek. "It cannot be helped."

KABLUK OF THE ESKIMO

The days passed into weeks and the weeks into months. The icy period of winter was on the wane. The time "When the seals have young" came and the village stirred into activity preparing for spring. Everything was going well, everyone was happy.

But I was as an evil man among the good. Within me was the true source of wickedness. It was the canker of discontent, of disgruntled restlessness. I was conscious of this, of what a misfit I was among these people of the North, when previously I had shared fully their simplicity and tranquillity. The war had taken everything worthy from within me. It had robbed me of the muscular strength and resilience and stamina which formerly had made me rejoice in the hard life of the Eskimos. The war had deprived me of my steady nerves, my control of feeling, my simplicity of thinking. The war had left my spirit scarred and mutilated.

One hope was left me—Akpek. I still trusted in the old chief with a childish faith. Implicitly I believed that Akpek could restore me to my former goodness of heart.

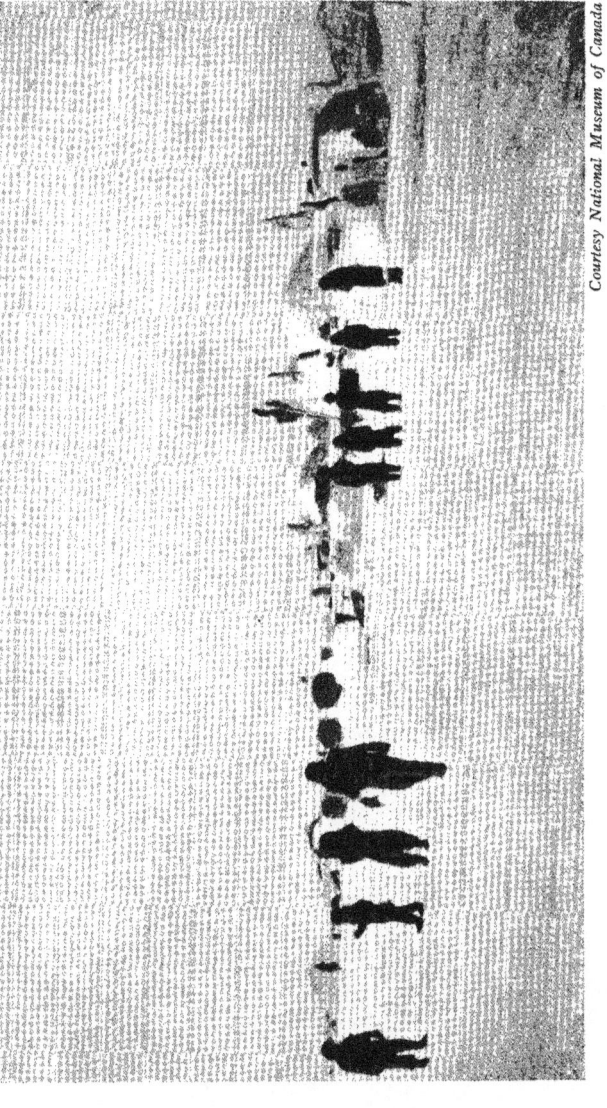

Courtesy National Museum of Canada

WHEN THE WAR WAS OVER I RETURNED TO AKPEK'S VILLAGE ON THE FRINGE OF THE FROZEN SEA

CHAPTER XXI

AKPEK, THE CHIEF, DEPARTS FOR AURORA BOREALIS

Akpek, the chief, wise in council and brave in the hunt, was ready to leave his people, to dwell for ever in the spirit land. The chief was very old and overnight he had become feeble. As spring came on, it was to be seen that he was dying.

An Eskimo, finding his usefulness gone, makes up his mind to die, and nothing can retard or prevent the fatal denouement. Akpek resigned himself to death. Neither the magic of the shaman nor the rudimentary medical skill I possessed was able to check his rapid descent to the grave. So far as my knowledge went, he was suffering from no organic disease.

I remained at his side.

The superstitious villagers believed that their chief's body was inhabited by Torngak, its familiar spirit, that it was responsible for the decay of Akpek; and if driven out and replaced by a more active and sympathetic spirit, the dying man would acquire a new lease of life.

To entice the familiar spirit outside of the body, the superstitious villagers called the sick man by another name; but it was in vain that his relatives and best friends saluted the chief, ostentatiously and loudly, by the new name of Amuk. The soul of the old man did not respond.

KABLUK OF THE ESKIMO

Old Nayume and Amaluke, their eyes filled with tears, pretended that there was nothing the matter with their lord, and, to deceive the familiar spirit, they laughed loudly. Their display of joyfulness, when their hearts were filled with bitter sorrow, was a most pathetic sight to witness. I comforted them as best I could.

The chief lay in his igloo, on his couch of caribou hides, without moving. At long intervals he would stir uneasily and mutter. By the third day it was evident that Akpek was about to die. Now that death was nigh, old Nayume and her daughter went to the igloo of relatives to await the end, according to custom.

In every igloo incantations were repeated without interruption for the safe journey to the spirit land. The long day drew to an end and I sat with the dying man, grief-stricken. With a sudden access of strength, Akpek endeavoured to raise himself into a sitting position. I sprang to his side and cushioned his back with a bundle of mink pelts.

"You are sad, my son," murmured Akpek.

"Aha, my father," I returned.

The chief paused and listened to the long wails of anticipatory mourning that came through the ice walls of the igloo as from a vast distance. His heart was grateful for the sincere marks of sympathy given by his people. His glance turned to me.

"Do not be sorrowful, my son," he said. "I have lived long. I am content to die."

AKPEK DEPARTS

"Aha, my father," I answered, with a voice that broke in spite of my efforts to hold it firm.

Akpek smiled faintly. There was a noise in the entrance and the curtain was thrust aside. Uyarak stuck his head into the chamber.

"The spirits of the air in the higher heavens are excited," he muttered in a low, restrained tone, and immediately withdrew.

I looked at the chief. He was filled with an unwonted animation; his arms moved restlessly, and his eyes gleamed brightly.

"The happy spirits of the departed are about to begin their dance in aurora borealis," he cried, with surprising strength.

"Aha, my father," I said, thinking that his mind was wandering.

"I must see aurora borealis once more," said Akpek.

Seeing that he was beyond aid in any case, I helped him down off the ice shelf; he crawled slowly through the entrance of the igloo into the open. His exertions so exhausted him that he could not stand and I propped him against the wall of the igloo.

Akpek's fast-fading eyes were held by the spectacle in the sky, the unforgettable spectacle of the aurora borealis. Emerging from the northern horizon was a timidly glowing cloud. All nature seemed to be waiting in quiet suspense under its flaky pall of snow and ice.

The sky was deep, blazing with the scintillation

of myriads of stars, and they appeared larger and of a more vivid brilliance because of the inky blackness of the infinite void. Innumerable coruscating diamonds they were, adorning the immense robe in which the firmament was wrapped. A soft phosphorescence illumined the sky and the white world below, enveloping the whole universe with a mystical glow. The great white silence of the Arctic, felt more by intuition than by the senses, reigned supreme.

As I watched, the peculiar luminous white cloud on the northern horizon grew. It advanced, swelled, stretching itself in its silent creeping march toward the zenith until the huge curtain covered half the sky, glowing with a mild phosphorescence through which the stars shone with tremendous brightness.

The edge of the luminous curtain passed overhead and burst into immense ribbons which formed gigantic convolutions with marvellous speed. Spires and streamers of glowing, vivid hues expanded and contracted, forming and reforming in unstable rosettes, gathered together without apparent aim, like a luminous transparent veil, dragging its fringes over the icy world beneath.

Akpek sat as though held in a trance. The ever-moving veil in the North shivered, seeming to billow under the soft breath of some mysterious zephyr; and the heavens were lit up by myriads of sparks of all of the colours of the rainbow. These magnificent celestial fires advanced and receded, gently mounted up and languidly dropped in graceful motion, softly shedding delicate colours, and, at

AKPEK DEPARTS

intervals, discharging innumerable rocket-like crystals of sparkling light.

Out of the impalpable curtain sharp points of coloured light pulsated, dancing fairylike everywhere, in a disordered harmony; jumping, turning, merging, melting and reappearing in delicate shades of blue, red, and green; a symphony of blended iridescence.

It seemed to me that I could touch those sharply tinged lights that filled the universe; I thought I could hear as well as see that symphony of luminosity. No sound could be detected by the ears, but I sensed a humming or soft hissing with my entire being, mental and physical.

Before my dazzled eyes, the aurora borealis had become a prodigious spectacle of incomparable grandeur and splendour, the magnitude of which no earthly words could interpret.

"My son. . . ." The words seemed to come to me from an immense distance. I turned to the chief. Under the eerie light, Akpek had taken on an added dignity, a dignity that was enhanced by the imminence of death. The ancient patriarch tried to speak again but the words did not come. With a tremendous effort he heaved himself to his feet and with his face turned upward he stood for a moment, his face bathed in the uncanny light.

I stood rooted to the ground. The chief's eyes closed; an ineffable smile curved the corners of his mouth; and, like a block of ice, he fell at my feet.

Akpek the chief was dead!

CHAPTER XXII

SO THE STORY ENDS

THE death of Akpek left me without hope. I had clung to him with a childish dependence and beside his grave I sobbed in intolerable sorrow. The world was a desolate abyss of pain and woe. I had lost the North and its magic for ever.

For the full six days of mourning I stayed at the village. I hated the place now, but after all I was "Kabluk of the Eskimo", and I acted according to custom. It was with ill-concealed relief that I finally hit the trail bound for "The Fort".

The trading post was much the same. The no-good "White Men" were still hanging around and a band of Naskopies was in from the interior. I was in bad spirits and I craved company when I had none, and solitude when there was anyone around. The men at the post sensed my moodiness and left me alone.

I had come to hate the North with its everlasting blanket of white snow and ice, its bleak rocks and crags, and its cruel insensate savagery. My nerves were in a bad way and I was on pins and needles to get out.

The ice went out early and the first ship to arrive

SO THE STORY ENDS

was a vessel belonging to the Hudson Bay Company. I asked the captain to take me out. He knew me by reputation and I went with him when he sailed. It was like the escape of a fugitive.

And so the story ends. Back in civilized parts I was regarded as a man expert in the ways of the North. The Hudson Bay Company employed me. I went to the west and promotion came rapidly. In almost no time at all I was an inspector, and in that capacity I travelled all over northern Canada, west of Hudson Bay.

I had little time to eat my heart out with vain longings, and when I camped after a hard day on the trail, my sleep was deep and dreamless. I moved swiftly and had no time to waste in vague repinings.

Years have sped by and the inaccessible North is inaccessible no longer. Others have travelled the formerly forbidden wastes. The tractor is supplanting the *komutik* and the kayak's place is being taken by fast motor-boats; but the chief factor in the opening up of the Arctic wastes is that annihilator of distance, the aeroplane.

In increasing droves people are travelling northward, traversing greater distances in a year than I have covered in my whole career, but they do not sense the great grandeur and mystery of the tundra country; they travel so fast that there is not sufficient time to grasp the significance of the land or to understand the soul of the Eskimo.

KABLUK OF THE ESKIMO

A disease gnaws the Arctic country, a disease that spreads and cannot be stopped; and that disease is civilization. Seemingly it brings peace and abundance to the dwellers of the great white wastes, but in truth it has destroyed the wonderful simplicity of the Eskimo people.

I often ask myself what Akpek, the chief, would have thought of the new order of things. Whether his people are happier with the glittering trinkets and shiny trifles brought with that irresistible canker, civilization. Or whether the old days with their quiet, even tenor were not to be preferred.

At such times, in my mind's eye, I can see the patriarchal old chief shake his head mournfully and can hear him grunt:

"*Emarha*—who knows?"

And then I shake my head too and murmur the words aloud with a sigh:

"*Emarha*—who knows?"

THE END

Hutchinson's
IMPORTANT NEW BOOKS FOR THE AUTUMN OF 1932

BIOGRAPHY AND MEMOIRS

The Life of Lord Oxford and Asquith

It is with great pleasure that we announce this authoritative and official life of the late Lord Oxford, which makes one of the most important publications of recent years.

Mr. Cyril Asquith tells the story of the early part of his brilliant father's life from its beginnings in Yorkshire, and Mr. J. A. Spender takes up the story from the formation of Sir Henry Campbell-Bannerman's Government in December 1905 and, with many intimate details, carries it to Lord Oxford's retirement from the leadership of the Liberal Party in 1926.   *In two volumes, Illustrated, £2 2s. the set.*

by
J. A. SPENDER AND CYRIL ASQUITH

Alfred Fripp

One of the leading surgeons of his day, professionally or socially Sir Alfred Fripp knew every famous figure of his times. In the Great War he was Consulting Surgeon to the Navy, and in his closing days he astonished the country by the energy he displayed in organizing the Frothblower movement.

Mr. Cecil Roberts has approached the man as a study of a personality that was a mixture of diffidence and courage, of introspection and high ambition, and who was, in all senses of the words, "the beloved physician".   *Illustrated, 18s.*

by
CECIL ROBERTS
Author of *Half Way*, *Spears Against Us* (7th Impression), etc.

BIOGRAPHY & MEMOIRS

Edgar Wallace

For seventeen years, first as his secretary and later as his wife too, Mrs. Wallace was in close association with every mood of Edgar Wallace. She knew him as well as it is possible for one human being to know another, and in this volume she traces the romantic career of her husband till the time of his death in Hollywood.

Illustrated, 12s. 6d.

by
HIS WIFE

Kaye Don: King of Speed

No man alive can claim more records in the world of motor-cycling, motor-racing, and motor-boating than Mr. Kaye Don, the only man who has travelled at two miles a minute, on land, in the air, and on the water.

He has looked on death in many forms, faced disasters, suffered injury and countless disappointments, and to-day is one of the most modest and self-effacing of all that gallant band of men whose lives are lived dangerously in order that mechanical science may progress.

Illustrated, 12s. 6d.

by
J. WENTWORTH DAY
Author of *Speed: The Life of Sir Malcolm Campbell*, etc.

The Whole Story

Here is the remarkable story of one of the most romantic figures of the stage. *Illustrated,* 12s. 6d.

by
"JUNE"
(Lady Inverclyde)

BIOGRAPHY & MEMOIRS

I Had Almost Forgotten . . .

In this volume Mr. Cochran talks with equal frankness about his successes and his failures, relishing a story against himself as hugely as one to his credit. And what a glittering procession of personalities passes in review! Royalties and peers, Cabinet Ministers and commoners, painters, singers, dancers and actors, producers and impresarios, box-office managers and stage-hands, prizefighters and the whole motley crowd of entertainers with their tantrums and their temperaments, their genius and their generosity, flash into Mr. Cochran's mirror.

Illustrated, 12s. 6d. net.

Random Revelations *by*
CHARLES B. COCHRAN
With an Introduction by A. P. HERBERT

With Northcliffe in Fleet Street

Sir John A. Hammerton, whose name appears on an immense list of Harmsworth publications as their editor, had peculiar opportunities of appreciating the character and amazing activities of Lord Northcliffe over a period of seventeen years.

Written in the frankest fashion and extremely outspoken about his faults and failings, this book presents Northcliffe in new and attractive aspects, and should be read by all interested in the literary and journalistic world of the last forty epoch-making years.

With a frontispiece, 10s. 6d.

by
J. A. HAMMERTON
Author of *Barrie: the Story of a Genius*

Other Weapons

This is the almost incredible story of a German who spent all the years of the War in an English Censor's Office.

Written with reserve and modesty, the book makes extraordinarily interesting and thrilling reading. It is the amazing story of how a man, playing a lone hand, and as fairly as possible under the circumstances, carried on his self-imposed mission from motives of patriotism. 12s. 6d.

by
J. C. SILBER
With a Foreword by Major-General LORD EDWARD GLEICHEN

BIOGRAPHY & MEMOIRS

Upheaval

Madame Woronoff is of the company who have seen all that once made their life swept ruthlessly away in the greatest upheaval the world has ever known. She has seen vast armies melt away like snow before the sun in that mysterious collapse of the valiant attempts to uphold the old order against the crimson tide of Bolshevism.

Simply, and without malice or bitterness, she recounts her almost incredible adventures: her husband's and her escapes from the Bolsheviks, her experiences whilst her husband joined the doomed White Armies, and at last their flight from Russia.   Illustrated, 12s. 6d.

by
OLGA WORONOFF
With an Introduction by BOOTH TARKINGTON

The Maid of the Mountains: Her Story
The Reminiscences of
JOSÉ COLLINS

Few actresses have had a more dramatic and spectacular career than the daughter of Lottie Collins of "Ta-ra-ra-boom-de-ay" fame, and her story promises to make one of the most interesting theatrical books for several years past.

The inside story of the "Maid of the Mountains" is one of the most remarkable chapters of theatrical history, and Miss Collins reveals it all in her book for the first time.   Illustrated, 12s. 6d.

Hell's Angels of the Deep

"Hell's Angels of the Deep" is Lieutenant Carr's own exciting story from the day, in 1911, when he ran away to sea, until the Armistice in 1918. Into those seven years Lieutenant Carr crammed an amazing variety of adventures, serving in every kind of vessel, enduring every sort of condition at sea, meeting hundreds of interesting people.   Illustrated, 10s. 6d.

by
LIEUTENANT WILLIAM GUY CARR
Author of By Guess and By God (13th impression)

HISTORY

The Concise Story of the Dover Patrol
Complete History of the Force

With his standard book on the Dover Patrol, published in 1919, Sir Reginald Bacon created a profound impression. In the words of the "*Daily Telegraph*", it was "*a revelation not only of the Admiral's own initiative and resourcefulness, his daring and his caution, but also of the adaptability of thousands of men of varied professions hailing from all parts of the kingdom to the hardships and perils of the exacting and arduous work they were called upon to perform in 'The Narrows'.*"

Thus Admiral Bacon's new volume is of the first importance, containing details and facts which will surprise and enthral the reader. It is the complete history of a singularly heroic force.

Illustrated, 12s. 6d.

by

ADMIRAL SIR REGINALD BACON, K.C.B., K.C.V.O., D.S.O.

With a Foreword by ADMIRAL OF THE FLEET EARL JELLICOE, O.M., G.C.B., G.C.V.O.

The Home Front

This notable and important book is a graphic presentment of life at home during the Great War; its labours, humours and sorrows, privations and bereavements. The author, who threw herself unreservedly into the work of relief and assuagement, writes from a store of unrivalled experience of the calling up of the men, the panic closing of the factories, the food prices rising to famine height, of food queues and profiteering, the munition girls and their hard toil, and of all the weariness of those dreadful years followed by the inevitable and difficult reactions of peace. There are also piquant and poignant reminiscences of many of the leading people of the time.

Illustrated, 18s. net

by

SYLVIA PANKHURST

HISTORY

The Romance of Lloyd's
From Coffee House to Palace

Here is a romantic and thrilling story of insurance which, linking sea and land in a world-wide net, has grown under the name of Lloyd's to be a corporation of the first importance and magnitude. To the ordinary man Lloyd's is a synonym for efficiency, but the reader is here taken far afield and is shown the ramifications whereby from the humblest beginnings in a London coffee house Lloyd's has become a household word from John o' Groats to the Horn.

Commander Worsley is the well-known hero of the "Endurance" and "Quest" fame, both of which ships he commanded.

Illustrated, 12s. 6d.

by

COMMANDER F. A. WORSLEY, D.S.O., O.B.E., R.N.R.,
In collaboration with CAPTAIN R. G. GRIFFITH

---

40 O.B., or How the War was Won

Secretary to the Director of Naval Intelligence, during the whole of the Great War, Mr. Hoy was in the closest possible touch with the innermost councils of the "Silent Service". His book is the first to reveal to the general public the true story of Britain's amazing salvation of the Allied Cause from German efficiency, and tells of the romantic Secret Service department of the Admiralty known as Room 40 O.B.

Illustrated, 15s.

by

H. C. HOY
Late Secretary to the Director of Naval Intelligence

TRAVEL

From Piccadilly to Devil's Island

This is the story of a traveller, and thus in his own words he sets forth his purpose in writing the book:

"Most of the countries in the world have left their stamp on my passport: from China in the East to Devil's Island in the West. It talks, that passport—of the glitter and heartbreak of Hollywood, of the queer narrow streets of Canton, of the pampas of the Argentine, of the silver sands of the South Sea Islands, the golden temples of Cochin China, and the night clubs of Paris. And, believe me, to land at St. Laurent du Maroni, French Guiana (Devil's Island), without letter of introduction or any form of permit, gives one quite a thrill."

Illustrated, 12s. 6d.

by
ARTHUR MILLS (the Novelist)

Little-Known Mexico
The Story of a Search for a Place

The Mexico of to-day—its little-known towns, its changeful landscapes, its manners and customs—become part of the reader's own experience in this vivid book. From the capital town down to the Guatemalan border, from the oilfields near Tampico to the Pacific port of Mazatlán, the author wanders, and as you accompany her you feel almost that you are in Mexico—so brilliantly does she write.

Illustrated, 12s. 6d.

by
MARIAN STORM

My Jungle Book

"My Jungle Book" is not merely the story of expeditions to remote parts of the countries watered by the Amazon and the Orinoco, but is as well the "credo" of an unconventional explorer. Full of verbal dynamite and written in a breezy, frank style, the book makes pungent remarks on Venezuelan politics, missionaries, Indians as compared with white men, and so forth.

Illustrated, 12s. 6d.

by
HERBERT S. DICKEY

NATURAL HISTORY

Close-Ups of Birds

The insight into the details of bird behaviour, which is only possible from the hide of a bird photographer, is shown in the information amassed by Mr. Southern, who has interwoven his own impressions of the beauty and fascination of his subject. We go with him after the lordly heron in some quiet Midland park ; after sea birds on the wild Welsh coast ; and we shiver with him in the icy blast of a north-easter watching wild duck. *Illustrated* 15s.

by
H. N. SOUTHERN
With a Foreword by SIR GERALD DU MAURIER

Snakes !

Mr. FitzSimons is famous as the Director of the celebrated Museum and Snake Park at Port Elizabeth, South Africa, and, known as "The Fabre of South Africa", he has studied and written about snakes all his life, and in this new book he tells of the many enthralling adventures which have befallen him and others in his work, and reveals many astounding facts. *Illustrated*, 12s. 6d.

by
F. W. FITZSIMONS, F.Z.S., F.R.M.S.
(Director of Port Elizabeth Museum and Snake Park)

The Practical Dog Book

It is claimed that this is the most wonderful and comprehensive dog book ever produced. It contains over 230,000 words and 500 illustrations. It has chapters on the Authentic History of all Varieties hitherto unpublished, and a Veterinary Guide and Dosage Section, and Information on Advertising and on Exporting to all Parts of the World.
Illustrated, 21s.

by
EDWARD C. ASH

SPORT

"To Whom the Goddess..."

Hunting and Riding for Women

Written by two women who have ridden and hunted all their lives, and whose knowledge of their subject is unquestionably profound, this book, though primarily intended for beginners, will appeal equally to those of experience. Based on the traditional aspect of hunting, it will be welcomed by all those who profess love for this fascinating subject, and it should find a place in every sporting library.

Illustrated, 15s.

by

LADY DIANA SHEDDEN AND LADY APSLEY

With an Introduction by the EARL OF LONSDALE, K.G.

Wings and Hackle

A Pot-pourri of Fly-fishing for Trout and Grayling and of Notes on Bird Life chiefly in Hampshire, Devon, and Derbyshire

Published in the first instance many years ago, "Wings and Hackle" attained instant recognition as a book of exceptional charm and instruction. To the original book a number of beautiful photographs have now been added, and its reappearance should be welcomed, not only by fishermen, but by all who find interest in the life of the riverside.

Illustrated, 7s. 6d.

by

RAYMOND HILL

POLITICS

England's French Dominion?

In this book Mr. Teeling shows the growing influence of the French Canadian and the French Catholic, and what it means; the dangers to the Prairie Provinces of Central European immigrants; the life in British settlements in the West, the unhappy lot of the unemployed and the deportees; and, in short, all the varied sides of life that make up the Canadian picture. With a frontispiece and map, 7s. 6d.

by
WILLIAM TEELING

FLIGHT

Down Africa's Skyways

Young and old alike will find a thrill in this story, so graphically told, of the aerial route to Africa. Starting with the epic flight of Van Ryneveld and Brand, the author introduces us to air pioneers who have blazed the trail which has enabled Imperial Airways to forge a giant aerial chain, linking London to Cape Town.
Illustrated, 10s. 6d.

by
BENJAMIN BENNETT

FINE ARTS

Pewter Down the Ages

In this imposing work Mr. Cotterell, the acknowledged authority upon pewter, takes us over many centuries of the Craft of the Pewterer, displaying in chronological sequence, from early mediæval to present times, typical examples of the pewterer's art, in a fine series of illustrations. Profusely illustrated, 21s.

by
HOWARD H. COTTERELL, F.R.Hist.Soc.
Author of *Old Pewter : Its Makers and Marks*, etc.
With a Foreword by F. Antonio de Navarro, F.S.A.

Announcing Important Cheap Editions

❖

Gladys Cooper
by
GLADYS COOPER

"*M*iss Cooper's gaiety and wit, her common sense and her intelligence are revealed on every page . . . should have a conspicuous success."—SUNDAY EXPRESS. *Illustrated*, 5s.

Secrets of Houdini
Authoritatively revealed for the first time *by*
J. C. CANNELL

"*K*eeps the reader gasping at every page . . . exhilaratingly uncanny."—SUNDAY TIMES.
"*A* book to have, to enjoy, and to keep."—SUNDAY GRAPHIC.
Illustrated, 3s. 6d.

Less than the Dust:
The Autobiography of a Tramp
by
JOSEPH STAMPER

"*T*here are pages with the quality of Maxim Gorki."—COMPTON MACKENZIE IN THE DAILY MAIL.
"*A* book worth all your best sellers . . . cuts right down to the bone of life."—DAILY HERALD. *With a frontispiece*, 3s. 6d.

How Animals Live
by
J. MOREWOOD DOWSETT

"*F*ascinating and spontaneous . . . drawn on by the spell of so much knowledge presented with so much zeal."—OBSERVER.
Illustrated, 7s. 6d.

Lauterbach of the China Sea
by
LOWELL THOMAS

"*I*rresistible to all lovers of romantic adventure."—NEWS-CHRONICLE.
"It is an amazing record."—SUNDAY TIMES.

Illustrated, 5s.

Twenty-nine Years :
The Reign of King Alfonso XIII of Spain
by
MRS. STEUART ERSKINE

"*F*or a student of Spanish affairs it is indispensable, and the ordinary reader will find it bristling with interest."—LEICESTER EVENING MAIL.

Illustrated, 5s.

A Yellow Sleuth
The Autobiography of "NOR NALLA" (Detective-Sergeant, Federated Malay States Police)

"*A* more enthralling volume of secret service could not be desired."—OBSERVER.

Illustrated, 3s. 6d.

Gamblers All
by
PHILIP SERGEANT

"*A*n entertaining medley relating to gaming and gamesters in many countries and many ages."—MORNING POST.

Illustrated, 3s. 6d.

Rooms of Mystery and Romance
by
ALAN FEA

"*N*ot to be taken to bed if you are sleeping alone in a moated grange."—DAILY EXPRESS.

Illustrated, 5s.

www.ingramcontent.com/pod-product-compliance
Lightning Source LLC
Chambersburg PA
CBHW020325170426
43200CB00006B/274